YOU'VE G

LAUGH

Sunday Morning Laughter
from Jack Shaw

The **Hallamshire** Press
1996

Published by The Hallamshire Press
The Hallamshire Press is an Imprint of
Interleaf Productions Limited
Broom Hall
8–10 Broomhall Road
Sheffield S10 2DR
England

Typeset by Interleaf Productions Limited
Printed in Great Britain by The Cromwell Press, Wiltshire

British Library Cataloguing in Publication Data
  A catalogue record for this book is available from the British Library

ISBN 874718 21 0

Happiness always...
Ken Dodd

Foreword

by Ken Dodd

LAUGHTER is the greatest sound in the world and I am delighted that this book will not only provide liberal doses of tickle-tonic, but also help raise vital funds for Christian Aid.

Laughter is a safety valve which airs the lungs and exercises the chuckle-muscles before reaching parts that no other human emotion can reach. And, it comes in various sizes: titters, giggles, belly-laughs and woofers!

There's nothing quite like a good woofer!!

So sit back and enjoy the humour contained in this book. Have a good laugh and help Christian Aid at the same time.

Always remember that it is important to laugh and smile as often as you can. Just imagine what a happier place the world would be if we all went around laughing our heads off!

I can only close by telling you that discovering I could make people laugh was like being kissed by an angel.

Keep laughing...

TATTY-BYE EVERYBODY, TATTY-BYE!!

Christian Aid
At Work in the World
We believe in life before death

The philosophy behind Christian Aid is that, whenever possible, people should be helped in such a way that they can then help themselves. For over 50 years, and in over 70 countries around the world, aid has been used to help self-sufficiency, often with low interest loans which can be repaid after profits or harvests, thereby helping poor people to earn an independent income.

Sometimes, of course, situations arise which are so devastating in their severity that emergency aid has to be provided. Yet even then, Christian Aid seeks to back schemes run by local people who know best what their communities need and how aid can be used effectively and quickly. Using 'partners' in this way prevents expensive administration and bureaucracy. Churches overseas play a huge part in this work, though *need* rather than *belief* is the only criterion used in the distribution of aid.

Christian Aid believes that charity is not enough, so it also campaigns for a better deal for the poor from banks, big business and governments. As Trevor McDonald has said, 'Christian Aid has an outstanding record in helping people in need around the world. It deserves the support of us all'.

For more information write to:
Christian Aid, PO Box 100, London, SE1 7RT
or telephone 0171 620 4444.

Registered charity no. 258003

Introduction

I was once a theological student and for four years my colleagues were mainly people who were studying to become Baptist ministers. On the whole they were very amusing people, with a nice line in wit and self deprecation. They were capable of doing the daftest of things, like one student who, on hearing that one of his colleagues was about to preach a 'hell and damnation' sermon in sermon-class, dragged a fire-extinguisher into the college chapel—just in case! On another occasion, at the same college, the Principal was quite ill and a well meaning student prayed earnestly for him in evening prayers 'O Lord wilt Thou *undertake* for our Principal'. In charge of the neighbouring Methodist college was Dr Norman Snaith and he had a reputation for being on intimate terms with the Almighty. It was an intimacy he carried into his prayers. So when one morning he began worship in the college chapel with the words 'Good morning Lord', a student, as quick as a flash, responded 'Morning Snaith!'

Perhaps it is the happy memory of those days that makes me look for humour amongst clergy today when so many seem to be overburdened with piety. It's almost a relief to read stories about people like the last Archbishop of Canterbury, Lord Runcie, who, shortly after a much publicised meeting with the Pope, was accused of being 'a Romaniser'. He was obviously irritated by the criticism until a colleague said, 'It could be worse—they could be calling you "a womaniser"'. I agree with Ken Dodd, laughter is the greatest sound in the world. A prayer in Chester Cathedral runs:

> *Give me a sense of humour Lord,*
> *Give me the power to see a joke,*
> *To find some happiness in life*
> *And pass it on to other folk.*

I like that prayer.

The stories in this book have come to me via the listeners of BBC Radio Sheffield's *Sunday Morning Breakfast Show*. One morning I said over the air that it would be nice if we could have a chuckle in the programme and I asked for a few 'churchy funnies'. The jokes have been arriving ever since, some unquotable but most full of whimsy and sometimes wisdom.

Obviously, some people in this world of ours don't find much to laugh about. Belly laughs must be difficult when your belly is empty and your life hangs by a thread. So, the publishers have offered to send 50 pence for every book sold to Christian Aid. Hopefully it will pay for a tool or two to aid the magnificent work they have been doing for 50 years in the poorest, neediest parts of the world.

I am grateful to the publishers Hallamshire Press, who, against all the commercial odds, continue to produce beautiful books, to Paul Rowland, an old student of mine, who drew the cartoons and to Ken Dodd who wrote the *Foreword*. Ken was in good form at the time because he had just heard that his Knotty Ash jam mines had struck a new marmalade seam! It wouldn't surprise me if clowns were one day numbered high in the Kingdom of Heaven—angels, archangels, Charlie Chaplin, Tommy Cooper, Bob Hope, Morcambe and Wise, Canon and Ball and Ken Dodd. Can you imagine the heavenly scene as they all gather round and say, 'Lord, tell us the one about the plank and the splinter!'

Jack Shaw
September 1996

Advertisements

ADVERTISEMENT in pets column of a local daily newspaper:
'FOR SALE—Kittens: mother Siamese; father cat-flap opportunist.
Ready now.'

BETHLEHEM: One star accommodation.
Self-catering only. Animals welcome.
Cot provided.

Trade-Off
Kittens, £1 each; call Ben.
Kittens, free; call Ben's Mum.

Or the advertisement for the Annual Parish Social which extended the following intriguing invitation:

Notice in Ads Column:
Small round table, old,
not reproductive.

'**Everyone welcome. Do come along if
you have nothing on and join in the fun.**'

3-Bed House, 2 WCs, No Chain

F. BLOGGS
DOUBLE GLAZING
TEL: 01101011

Holy Orders
In the employment section
of a local paper: 'Position
requires wisdom of
Solomon, patience of Job,
skill of David. No other
applicants have a prayer.'

When I asked you to leave your mark
on the church I hadn't got this in mind!

Announcements

Vicar at P.C.C. Meeting: 'Would anyone like the visiting Missionary for lunch on Monday?'

On a New York convalescent home: 'For the sick and tired of the Episcopal Church'

'The ladies have cast off clothing of every kind, and they can be seen in the church basement on Friday afternoon.'

At the end of his 'notices' the church secretary said: 'Will the lady who left her watch in the church hall last week please claim it in the vestry after the service.' Immediately afterwards, the minister announced: 'We shall now sing hymn number 123—*Lord her watch Thy church is keeping.*'

In a Pennsylvania cemetery: 'Persons are prohibited from picking flowers from any but their own graves.'

'It's good news and bad news,' said Moses, as he came down Mount Sinai, 'I've got the list down to ten but adultery is still in!'

'At the choir concert on Thursday, Mrs Ida Penny will sing 'Put me in a little wooden bed', accompanied by the vicar.'

Announced in a church one Sunday: The preacher for Sunday next will be found hanging on the notice board in the porch.

'Robin Smith has asked me to draw your attention to the raffle tickets on sale in aid of the Unmarried Mothers' Society, for whom he is directly responsible.'

Jumble Sale next Saturday morning. This is a good chance to get rid of anything not worth keeping. Why not bring your husband?

Aphorisms

Consider the postage stamp: its usefulness consists in the ability to stick to one thing till it gets there.

Conceit *is a form of I-strain.*

Money *is the loot of all evil.*

A clear conscience *is a result of a bad memory.*

Sales resistance *is the triumph of mind over natter.*

Women *are the weepier sex.*

Comic relief *is when the life of the party goes home.*

An egotist *is one who is always Me-deep in conversation, or a conceited ass who thinks he knows as much as you do.*

Childish games *are those at which your wife beats you.*

A bigot *is a person who just won't believe you are right.*

A self-made man *is a bad example of unskilled labour.*

Patience *is the ability to put up with people you would rather put down.*

Politics *is the art of foretelling what will happen tomorrow, next month, next year, and being able to explain why it didn't happen.*

A beautiful woman *is one you notice.* **A charming woman** *is one who notices you.*

Life *is what happens when you are making other plans.*

Like a piano you may not be grand, but you can be upright.

If you don't live as you believe, then you begin to believe as you live.
The Hadith

Army

Seated beside a senior officer at an army dinner, a young subaltern tried to open the conversation. 'Do you ride, sir?' 'No. Tried it once, didn't like it,' was the only reply.

Later the young man tried again. 'Ever go to the opera, sir?' 'No. Tried it once, didn't like it,' the great man snapped once more. Then, attempting to be more sociable, he added, 'You look about the same age as my son.' 'Your only son, sir?'

Baptisms

Believers' Baptism doesn't seem
as popular as it used to be

**Vicar at Baptism: 'Why do you name the child after me?
Are you going to make a parson of him?'
'No,' replied the father, 'he'll have to work for his living.'**

*'Why does the Vicar put a cross on the foreheads of the babies he has baptised?' asked the little girl.
'So he knows which ones he's done, silly!' retorted her brother.*

An Irishman making application for Social Benefit went to fill in a form. The officer in charge offered to do it for him asking, 'What is your name?' The Irishman replied 'Patrick, Terrence, O'Dear, O'Sullivan'.

The officer repeated slowly: 'Patrick, Terrence, O'Dear your third name is very unusual, some family connection I suppose?'

Irishman: 'Oh no, nothing like that, after the second name he dropped me in the font'.

The Vicar announced at a PCC meeting that he was going to install a second font near the chancel steps so that he could baptise babies at both ends.

Could you do the other end as well vicar?

Two vicars, over coffee one morning, discover that both their churches are infested with bats.

'Once I got so cross' said the first 'that I tried to shoot them. I made some holes in the roof but did nothing to the bats.'
'I tried catching them' said the second, 'then I drove 50 miles before releasing them but they beat me back to the church.'
They contacted the Diocesan expert.
His advice:
'Baptise them. Then you'll be sure not to see them again!'

In a black gospel service a beautiful young girl called Lisa was about to be baptised by total immersion.
'Before I baptise you,' said the minister, 'how about a word of testimony?'
'Last night,' said the girl, 'I was in the arms of the devil. Tonight I'm in the arms of the Lord.'
Just then a voice from the back of the church said, 'How's yer fixed for tomorrow night, Lisa?'

'Name this child,' said the Vicar at the baptism.
'Tia Maria, Vicar,' said the father.
'Tia Maria?' protested the Vicar. 'You can't seriously intend calling this poor girl Tia Maria!'
'Well actually we wanted to call her Martini originally,' explained the mother. 'The only trouble is, she still isn't dry enough.'

Beatitudes

Blessed are those who can laugh at themselves.
They will have no end of fun.
Blessed are those who can tell a mountain from a molehill.
They will be saved a lot of bother.
Blessed are those who know how to relax without looking for excuses.
They are on the way to becoming wise.
Blessed are those who know when to be quiet and listen.
They will learn a lot of new things.
Blessed are those who are sane enough not to take themselves too seriously.
They will be valued by those about them.
Happy are you if you can take small things and face serious things calmly.
You will go far in life.
Happy are you if you can appreciate a smile and forget a frown.
You will walk on the sunny side of the street.
Happy are you if you can be kind in understanding the attitudes of others.
You may be taken for a fool but this is the price of charity.
Happy are you if you know when to hold your tongue and smile.
The Gospel has begun to seep into your heart.
Blessed are those who think before acting and pray before thinking.
They will avoid many blunders.
Above all—
Blessed are those who recognise the Lord in all whom they meet.
The light of truth shines in their lives.
They have found true wisdom.

Bestsellers

Short Grass by Moses Lawn

Feed your Dog by Nora Bone

Accident on the Cliff by Eileen Dover

How to get Rich by Robin Banks

Music for Christmas by Chris Tingles

Plants in Pots by Tom Artoe

Summers Here by June Days

Spring Rain by April Showers

White Hedgerows by May Blossom

Giving Thanks by Grace Beforemealz

Bird Watching by Jenny Wren

Full Assurance by May B. Knott

The Protestant Work Ethic by Daly Grind

The German Charismatic Movement by Hans Reising

Pray Continually by Neil Aylott

Salt of the Earth by Pastor Pepper

Intercession by Frank and Ernest Pleeding

Praise in the USA by Hal E. Looyah

End of the Week by Gladys Friday

Apologising Made Simple by Thayer Thorry

How to Get There by Ridya Bike

Army Jokes by Major Laugh

The Flower Garden by Polly Anthus

The Case of the Missing Conker by Nick McConker

Cookery for Beginners by Egon Chips

'Sir, failing to find any religious books in a local bookshop, I asked an assistant for help. She showed me an inconspicuous handful of Bibles and prayer books, saying, 'We have had to move them down to the bottom shelf because of Christmas.'

Bible

A lady was posting a gift of a Bible to her god-daughter. The counter clerk examined the heavy parcel and asked if it contained anything breakable. 'Nothing', she replied, 'except the Ten Commandments.'

The curate was convinced of the importance of involving the congregation in the Family Service Sermon. 'Who was the funniest man in the Bible?' he asked.

A teenager promptly replied, 'Samson. He brought the house down.'

One man believed that the best way to read the Bible was to open it at random and the verse his eye fell on was his inspiration for the day. That was until he opened up one day and read: 'He went out and hanged himself'.

'That can't be right', he thought, 'I'll try again.' This time his eye fell on: 'Go and do thou likewise'.

Somewhat shaken he tried again and read, 'What thou hast to do, do quickly'.

All life is in the Bible including the sporting activity of King David. He played tennis because we read, 'David served in the courts of Saul', and he must have had a motor-bike because we read, 'David's Triumph was heard throughout Israel.'

Bishops

At a confirmation service one small boy was so puzzled by a line on the 'Order of Service' sheet that he turned to his mother and asked" 'Why do we need to know the Bishop's address?'

A Yorkshire bishop detected one of his servants in a lie. 'You know my man,' he said, 'one far greater than either of us notices everything we do.' 'Yes, my Lord Bishop,' replied the man, 'she's already spoken to me about it.'

An unusual club partner?

The last time a Bishop visited us, a small boy in the congregation was very impressed when the Bishop explained all about the shepherd's crook and the significance of it.

The next day at school the boy told his teacher, 'We had the Bishop at church yesterday and now we all know what a crook looks like!'

After taking tea with a parishioner, the Bishop said, 'I'm glad to see how comfortably you are living.'
'Oh, Bishop,' replied the man, 'if you want to know how we really live, you must come when you're not here.'

She's trying to impress the Bishop

Bureaucracy

The Lord's Prayer has 58 words.
The Ten Commandments have 297 words.
The American Declaration of Independence has 310 words.
The EC Directive on the exporting of duck eggs has 28,911 words.

Catholics

In our parish the convent of the Sisters of Saint Francis is across the road from a Franciscan monastery. One day the nun at the switchboard heard: 'Sister, this is Brother. Father wants to talk to Mother.'

When asked by a visiting dignitary how many people actually worked in the Vatican, the Pope replied: 'About fifty per cent of them.'

I noticed our four-year-old daughter sitting on the floor, staring at her toe, so I asked what was wrong. 'Mum,' she replied thoughtfully, 'I think I have Catholic's foot.'

A priest looking through the window of his house was convinced he saw the Lord walking through the centre of the village. He was so concerned he phoned the Vatican and immediately got through to the Pope.
'I'm sure it's Jesus,' he said, 'What shall I do?'
The Pope replied, 'Look busy!'

Murphy was in the confessional and he said, 'Father, I've sinned. For years I've been stealing wood from work and I feel bad about it.
'Right', said the priest, 'Can you make a novena?'
'Certainly', said Murphy, 'if you have the plans, I've got the wood!'

A young girl at confession said to the priest: 'Father I've committed the most terrible sin. I look into the mirror and say to myself...Molly you're the prettiest girl in all the world.'
The priest replied: 'Get away with you Molly! That's not a terrible sin. That's just a mistake'.

Children in Church

During the church service my niece asked to go outside as she didn't feel well. She returned a few minutes later and admitted, 'I have been a little sick, but it doesn't matter, there's a little box at the door marked 'for the sick'.

At Sunday School, the preacher asked who would like to go to Heaven. Everyone put their hand up, except one boy and one girl. The preacher asked them why not and the girl replied: 'Mum told us to come straight home.'

A Vicar was astonished to hear little Mary say that a person must be brave to go to church. 'Well,' she said, 'I heard my uncle tell my aunt last Sunday that there was a canon in the pulpit, that the choir murdered the anthem, and that the organist drowned the choir.'

A small girl and boy were talking one Sunday. She said: 'They always say "amen" but never "a women"'.
'Don't be silly,' said her brother, 'that's because they are hymns!'

One day in Sunday School, the subject was the Ten Commandments, and the class had reached the last one. When the teacher asked if anyone could state what the tenth commandment was, young Donald waved his hand wildly, then proudly stood up and gave his answer: 'Thou shalt not take the covers off thy neighbour's wife.'

The Sunday School teacher asked her class 'What does the story of David and Goliath teach us?' Tommy replied, 'Please Miss, TO DUCK!'

Will the Youngsters Buy this New Image Vicar?

A child hearing the story of the Prodigal Son for the first time: 'In the midst of all the celebration for the prodigal,' said the teacher, 'there was one for whom the feast brought no joy, only bitterness. Can you tell me who it was?'
'The fatted calf?' suggested an unhappy little voice.

The Sunday School class had been told the story of the infant Moses. The teacher ended dramatically, 'Now whom do you suppose the Egyptian princess found to care for the little boy found in the bulrushes?'
Without hesitation came the answer: 'A babysitter.'

A small boy learned to play the cornet in the village band and was asked to play a solo in the chapel concert. When he got home his father asked: 'How did you get on son?' The boy replied: 'I don't think I did very well Dad. They asked me to play it again.'

When teaching a young Sunday School class the story of Lot's wife looking back and turning into a pillar of salt, one young boy said: 'That's nothing. My mum was out in the car with us and she looked back and turned into a telegraph pole.'

During a particularly long service a small voice was heard asking: 'Mummy, is it still Sunday?'

Young Irish boy's favourite Bible story: Jesus healing the 10 leprechauns!

The Sunday School teacher was trying to introduce her class to the world hallelujah. 'What special, unusual word do people of the church shout out with joy?' she asked.
'Bingo', one boy replied.

'Daddy, what's that?' said the little boy, looking up form the pew at the memorial plaque on the wall. 'That's in memory of all the brave men who died in the services.'
The little boy scanned the long list of names awe-struck and asked, 'Did they die in the morning or evening services?'

A local mother was slightly puzzled when her small daughter asked for a cucumber to take to Sunday School, but complied.
When the girl returned she confessed: 'Sorry Mum, got it wrong. We were supposed to bring a newcomer.'

Children at Home

You can tell when your kids are growing up. They stop asking you where they came from and start refusing to tell you where they're going.

For the first few years you teach your children to walk and talk. Then you spend your time telling them to sit down and shut up.

A child whose grandfather had just died ran in and asked, 'Where's Grandad?'
Her mother told her that he had gone to Heaven, to which the child replied: 'Well, he must have gone by bus because his car is still in the garage.'

One day when a minister and his wife were entertaining friends, their son John came in from playing to join them for a meal. He was immediately dispatched to the bathroom to wash his hands. 'You know what I keep saying about germs, Johnnie,' said his mother.
From outside the dining room door, a little voice was clearly heard to mutter, 'Germs and Jesus. It's all I hear about in this house and I've never seen either.'

Father to son: 'I don't care if the outside wall is cracked. Stop telling everyone you come from a broken home.'

Our four-year-old son came into the house to show me a caterpillar that was crawling up his arm. Trying hard to conceal my squeamishness, I said casually, 'Mark, why don't you take the caterpillar outside?' His mother will be looking for him.

I was feeling rather pleased at the way I had handled the situation when Mark came back into the house a few minutes later with two caterpillars and said excitedly, 'Look! I found the mother.'

I've Joined 'Friends of the Earth' Mam!

'Mummy, where did I come from?' the little girl asked one day on returning from school. Taking this as a golden opportunity, the young mother proceeded to explain the facts of life to her daughter. After some time, and some strange faces from the little girl, she piped up. 'Thanks, Mummy, I wanted to know because there is a new girl in our class and she says she comes from Edinburgh.'

The mother of a four-year-old boy struggling to get him into a pair of leggings said, 'James, lift up your leg', to which the child promptly replied: 'We lift them up unto the Lord.'

'Grandad, Grandad! Can I borrow your old tin-hat please?'
'What do you want that for lad?'
"It's for school Grandad—exhibition for V.E. Day.'
'Yes. OK then, though it will need cleaning up a bit.'
'Thanks Grandad. Is there anything else I could take?'
'I've got an old greatcoat somewhere.'
'What's a greatcoat?'
'It keeps you warm. I think it's in the loft I took it up years ago and wrapped it round the tank.'
'Wow! Grandad. Have you really got a tank up there?'

A woman had her three-year-old grandson to stay overnight. That evening there was a thunderstorm with spectacular flashes of lightening, so she went along to his bedroom to reassure him. The little boy was sitting up in bed, looking excited. 'Nanna,' he cried, 'God has just taken my photo.'

I want my children to have all the things I could never afford. Then I want to move in with them.
Phyllis Diller, quoted in *National Enquirer*

Rules of the Roost
Children certainly brighten up a home. Whoever saw a child under 12 turn off an electric light?

Children at School

Smile

Awhile

The infants' teacher held up a pair of gloves and asked, 'Whose are these?'
A small boy piped up, 'They look like mine, Miss.'
'So they are yours, are they William?'
'No, Miss, they can't be mine 'cos mine are lost!'

She won't sing. She says it's sexist.

John had been at school for a very short time.
'What have you learned?' said his mother one night.
He replied, 'If I had four apples and you gave me three more, I should have seven.'
'Well, smiled his mother, 'If I had four bananas and I gave you three more, how many would you have then?'
'Oh,' said John looking blank, 'we haven't done bananas yet.'

A schoolboy once wrote in his essay on lying. 'A lie is an abomination unto the Lord, but a very present help in trouble.'

'Ee our lad's been put into a class for backward readers. Ah reckon he must be clever to be able to read backwards, 'cos that's more than ah can do missen'.

On a school report:
Last year Jason hit rock-bottom.
This year he started drilling.

The following are quotes from essays written by American school children on classical music:
'Refrain means don't do it. A refrain in music is the part you'd better not try to sing.'
'Music sung by two people at the same time is a duel.'
'Henry Purcell is a well known musician few people have ever heard of.'

Anybody else want a stab at
the names of the Disciples?

A primary school teacher asked the class to solve this mathematical problem: 'Suppose you had £0.99 and your friend had £99: what would be the difference?'
'The dismal point." said one child.

An American schoolmistress returned from a visit to England and was telling her pupils of some of the wonderful sights she had seen. She referred to Lincoln Cathedral. 'Is there a Lincoln Cathedral in England?' asked one of the girls. 'Certainly there is and it is one of the most beautiful of all', was the reply. 'Say!' exclaimed the girl, 'Wasn't it just sweet of them to name it after him.

'Who knocked down the walls of Jericho?' the teacher asked young Jack.
'It wasn't me Miss', said Jack.
When Jack's mother picked him up from school the teacher told her what he'd said.
'Well', said the mother, 'if Jack says it wasn't him I believe him!'
Later that week the teacher saw Jack's father and told him the story.
'Don't let's make a fuss', he said, pulling a wad of notes from his pocket, 'How much will it cost to get it fixed!'

Choirs

'Owing to the illness of the tenor, the choir will sing
Beethoven's Ode to Joy.'

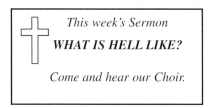

This week's Sermon

WHAT IS HELL LIKE?

Come and hear our Choir.

A choirmaster trying to inject some life into his sullen band at a rehearsal, asked them to repeat the hymn, 'Little drops of water, little grains of sand,' and, giving them the note said, 'Right, one more time—Little drops of water— and for goodness sake put some spirit in it!'

Singer: 'Now that you've heard my voice, whom do you suggest to accompany me?'
Impresario: 'A bodyguard.'

Choirmaster: Syncopation is the rapid movement between bars!

Christians

Some Christians are wise, some otherwise.

A Christian is an 'odd number'. He feels supreme love for one whom he has never seen. He talks familiarly every day to someone he cannot see, expects to go to heaven on the virtue of another, empties himself in order that he might be full, admits he is wrong, so he can be declared right, goes down in order to get up.

> The definition of 'Pillars of the Church' (of which the Church of England has many!): They hold everything up and obscure vision.'

He is strongest when he is weakest, richest when he is poorest, happiest when he feels worst. He dies so that he might live, forsakes in order to have, gives away so he can keep, seeks the invisible, hears the inaudible and knows that which passeth all knowledge.

At a church meeting a heated discussion was being held about changing the church name from 'Puddlington C of E Church' to 'The Puddlington Christian Church.' One dear old man stood up and said, 'I've been coming to this church for fifty years and nobody's going to start calling me a Christian!'

Some delegates to a Church Conference in Scotland set off between sessions to explore the countryside. They came to a stream spanned by a rickety bridge, and started to cross, ignoring the warning to 'Keep Off'.

A local inhabitant ran after them to protest. Not understanding his concern one of the visitors said, 'It's all right we are Anglicans from the Conference'.

'I'm not caring about that', was the reply, 'but if ye dinna get off the bridge ye'll all be Baptists.'

Christmas

A group of junior children were performing a Nativity play. They had been encouraged to improvise and use their own words. Two shepherds approached the manger nervously, smiled at Mary, and shyly knelt down without a word. The third, a bolder boy, looked into the manger, turned to Mary with a smile and said: 'Isn't he like his dad'.

'I don't know who she is
but she certainly packs 'em in...'

'What did you do on Christmas Eve?' the teacher asked. One lad, the son of a Vicar, said the family had been to church then opened their presents and sung a carol. A Roman Catholic girl told a similar story. she had been allowed to stay up late to attend Mass, after which friends had called in for a drink and everyone had sung carols. But a Jewish boy, whose father owned a toy factory, said: 'We went down to dad's works, looked at the empty shelves and then sang "What a friend we have in Jesus".'

Next year—No real donkeys. Right!

In a Nativity play rehearsal the young storyteller described the scene in the stable of Mary nursing the baby Jesus, while Joseph sat and watched the angel hoovering around them.

Two sisters were looking at a book of religious pictures and came across a painting of the Virgin and the baby Jesus.
'See,' said the older girl, 'that's Jesus, and that's his mother.'
'Where,' the younger girl wanted to know, 'is his father?'
Her sister thought for a moment, then explained, 'Oh, he's taking the picture.'

The Sunday School children were asked to draw a picture of the Nativity. One little girl drew Mary, Joseph, the baby Jesus in the manger, and an enormously fat man.
'Whoever is that?' asked the teacher.
'Oh,' the girl replied, 'That's Round John Virgin!'

Can't be too careful round here officer.

Christmas Cards

*I have a list of folks I know, all written in a book
And every year at Christmas time I go and take a look.
And that is when I realise that these names are a part
Not of the book they're written in, but of my very heart.
For each name stands for someone who has crossed my path sometime
And in that meeting, they've become the 'rhythm of the rhyme'.
And while it sounds fantastic for me to make this claim,
I really feel I am composed of each remembered name.
And while you may not be aware of any special link,
Just meeting you has shaped my life, more than ever you can think.
For once you've met somebody, the years cannot erase
The memory of a pleasant word, or of a friendly face.
So never think my Christmas card is just a mere routine
Of names upon a Christmas list, forgotten inbetween.
For when I send a Christmas card that is addressed to you,
It's because you're on that list of folks that I'm indebted to.
For you are but a total of the many folks I've met,
And you happen to be one of those I prefer not to forget.
And whether I have known you for many years or few,
In some way you have had a part in shaping things I do.
And every year when Christmas comes, I realise anew
The biggest gift that life can give is meeting folks like you.
So may the spirit of Christmas, that for ever more endures,
Leave its richest blessing in the hearts of you and yours.*

They sent us that Christmas card last year.

Church Going

A mechanically minded Methodist motorist wrote: 'After a Church service I expect to find: my battery charged, my brakes adjusted, my steering corrected, my engine tuned, my front and rear vision clear, and to run more smoothly.

The American cleric, Henry Ward Beecher was handed a note one Sunday morning before the service.
It contained a sing word: *fool*.
Mr Beecher described the note to his congregation.
'I have known many instances of a man writing a letter and forgetting to sign his name.' he said, 'but this is the first case I have ever known of a man signing his name and forgetting to write the letter.'

Finally About the Roof Fund...!

If you should find the perfect Church
Without one fault or smear,
For goodness sake, don't join that church,
You'd spoil the atmosphere.
But since no perfect church exists
Where people never sin,
Let's cease in looking for that church,
And love the one we're in!

The vicar shook hands with his parishioners and watched them hurry off down the road to the 'Pig and Whistle'.
'Why is there a headlong rush for the pub after Evensong?' he asked.
'Well', replied the curate, 'I suppose you could call it thirst after righteousness'.

A churchwarden escorted parishioners to their seats before the service. When two strangers arrived he greeted them and asked them where they would like to sit.
Confused, the young man smiled and answered, 'non-smoking please'.

A man attended church one Sunday and refused to remove his hat despite requests from many officials. Asked by the Minister after the service to explain his actions he replied, 'More people have spoken to me this morning than in the six months I have been coming here.'

The vicar saw one of his congregation heading for the river with a rod over his shoulder.
'I hope you're not fishing on a Sunday', said the vicar.
'It's alright for you', said the fisherman, 'Your dinner is in the oven, mine's still in the river.'

When you were born your mother brought you here
When you were married your wife brought you here
When you die your friends will bring you here
Why not try coming on you own sometimes.

Clergy

Loyal wife to callers who wanted to speak to the golf-playing Vicar: 'I am sorry, the Vicar is away on a course.'

A group of deacons began to get worried about their minister, who every day before breakfast would rush down to a railway siding to watch the Inter-City as it sped towards London.

Eventually, one deacon approached the minister and explained their concern.

'Don't be concerned,' said the minister, 'I just like looking at something that moves without me having to push it!'

A Clergyman—a keen cricketer—was concerned over whether or not cricket was played in heaven. He prayed that he may have a vision in order to find out. His prayer was answered, an angel appeared to him in a dream. The angel said: 'yes, the good news is cricket is played in heaven, the bad news is, you are in the team for next week.'

A South London clergyman appointed to another living received a letter from a firm of furniture removers. It stated, 'In the last year we have removed forty South London clergymen to the satisfaction of all concerned.'

The Vicar visited the old lady after Christmas, and while he was there he was offered a plate of nuts. A few weeks later he visited again and was offered some nuts once more. But he noticed that she didn't have one.

'No,' she said, 'People keep sending me boxes of chocolates, and I like chocolate but I don't like nuts, but I know you do.'

A card on the mat read,
'The vicar has called and found you out.'

A vicar was visiting a maternity ward and cooing over the new-born babies. One mother asked, 'Have you got any children Vicar?'
'No, no,' he replied, 'I'm afraid my stipend's far too small.'
Oh Vicar!' she said, 'I didn't realise you had a medical condition.'

The rector on seeing a small boy trying to reach a doorbell said, 'Let me help you sonny.' The rector gave a good ring. The boy looked at him and said, 'Now mister run like mad.'

The minister was visiting an elderly lady and agreed to pray with her that she might have better health. They knelt together on the floor and he began. 'Dear Lord, if it be your will restore Mrs. McIlroy to her former health.' He felt a touch on his arm, 'Excuse me,' said the lady, 'Call me Lizzie, he won't know me by my married name.'

A clergyman was driving his sports car at a fast pace. He had to scream to a standstill to avoid an accident. When the angry driver of the other car stormed over to exchange words, the vicar handed him his card:
'The Rev. Paul Brown is sorry to have missed you. He hopes to make contact with you next time.'

The Vicar is on his bike and the policeman puts up his hand to stop him. Squeal of brakes and the Vicar just manages to pull up in time. 'Nearly got you that time', said the policeman. 'You'll never get me, Constable; you see God is with me; God is always with me.' 'Ah, that's it. Got you this time, Vicar', says the policeman. 'Two on a bike.'

Collections

Take my silver and my gold
Not a mite would I withhold
But as times are rather hard,
Please accept my Barclay Card.

Sorry! I'm right out, just been to Tescos.

The churchwarden of Brampton Parish Church, Rotherham
wrote in the parish magazine for April Fools Day:
*'for a trial period of three months a new method of collecting the
offertory will be tried. The congregation will stand and the organist
will play a selection of hymns while the plate is passed around. When
the music stops whoever is holding the plate will place a five pound
note on it and sit down. This will continue until everyone is seated. It
should take no more than ten minutes. Thank you for your co-operation.'*

OK buster, lets see
a few readies!

Committees

Oh give me your pity! I'm on a committee
Which means that from morning 'til night
we attend and amend, and contend and
defend without a conclusion in sight.
We confer and concur, we defer and demur
and reiterate all of our thoughts,
we revise an agenda with frequent addenda
and consider a load of reports.
We compose and propose, we support and
oppose and the points of procedure are fun,
but though various notions are brought up as
motions there's terribly little gets done!

A committee is…a collection of the unfit chosen from amongst the unwilling by the incompetent to do the unnecessary.

You said the Committee Meetings Were Boring!

As a member of any church committee will tell you,
after all is said and done, there's a lot more said than done.

If Moses had called a committee the Jews would still be in Egypt.

Did you hear about the vicar who vetoed the request by the PCC for a chandelier in church. He explained, 'I would have to write the order for it and I can't spell the word and furthermore we have no-one in the parish who can play it, and what the church wants more than anything else is a new set of lights.'

Conference: A gathering of important people who singly can do nothing, but together can decide that nothing can be done.

Committee: A group that keeps minutes but loses hours.

Cops and Robbers

The Mexican bandit who robbed a Texas bank was apprehended on a busy street by an American police officer a few days later. The officer spoke no Spanish and the Mexican spoke no English, so a passing Mexican was asked to be the interpreter.

A thief, surprised by the returning householder as he attempted to break into a house in Carlisle, hid by swathing himself in the wet washing which hung on the line in the garden. He then coolly proceeded to a neighbouring house, broke in and stole a spin drier. He got clean away.

The officer poked a gun in the Mexican's belly and said to the interpreter, 'Ask him if his name is Manuel Gonzales.'

The interpreter said, 'He says, si, he was and he admits he robbed the bank.'

The officer pushed harder on the gun. 'Now tell him,' he said, 'I'm going to pull the trigger if he doesn't tell me where the money is.'

With sweat pouring down his face, the thief stammered in Spanish. 'Don't shoot! I've got a wife and four kids at home. The money is in the well behind the house.'

The interpreter said, 'he says you one big mouth. You no scare him! Go ahead and shoot!'

This is Joe.
He's a conscientious objector,
he doesn't want to fight,
he doesn't want to shoot,
he doesn't want to kill,
he doesn't want to drop bombs.
So we put him in jail.
'Why?'
'Because he's a threat to society.'

Did you hear the tale about the burglar who broke into a vicarage in the middle of the night? He disturbed the vicar who woke with a start and demanded to know what the intruder wanted.
'Stay where you are,' ordered the burglar. 'I'm hunting for your money.'
Let me get up and turn on the light,' said the vicar, 'and I'll hunt with you.'

Creation

Every 24 hours:
Your heart beats 103,680 times.
Your blood travels 43 million miles.
You inhale 438 cubic feet of air and
You digest 3 pounds of food.
You evaporate 2 pounds of water by perspiration and
You generate 450 tons of energy and
You use 750 muscles.
Your blood circulates your body every 32 seconds
and you use 7 million brain cells.
The bible says: I will praise thee; for I am fearfully
and wonderfully made. (Psalm 139:14)

We are all cast in the same mould; but some are mouldier than others.

'If I understand you correctly,' said the student, after the professor had explained the big-bang theory of the creation of the universe, 'first there was nothing and then it exploded.'

When the Creator was making the world, he told man he was giving him 20 years of normal sex life. Man was unhappy about this and asked for more—but was refused.
The monkey was then offered 20 years. 'I don't need 20,' protested the monkey. 'Ten will do.'
'May I have the extra ten years?' pleaded man, and this time the Creator graciously agreed.
Then he offered the noble lion 20 years. The lion didn't want more than ten either, so man asked for the surplus and was granted ten more years.
The donkey was offered 20 years but said ten was ample. Man again begged for the spare ten years and got them.
This perhaps explains why man has 20 years of normal sex life, ten years of monkeying around, ten years lion about it and ten years of making an ass of himself.

Creatures Great and Small

After his cat got stuck in a tree, a minister from South Africa mounted a rescue operation. He climbed a ladder as far as he could, tied one end of a rope to the narrow trunk then tied the other end to his car bumper.

As he drove forward, intending to bring the bough down far enough for the cat to jump off, the inevitable happened—the rope broke, catapulting the moggy into space.

No more was heard of the poor creature until a couple of weeks later. The minister was in the supermarket when he saw one of his church members buying cat food. 'I didn't know you had a cat', he said enquiringly. 'I didn't. It's a funny story, quite a miracle really. About two weeks ago I was having a picnic on the lawn with my daughter. 'I'd like to have a cat, Mummy,' she said. 'You'll have to ask Jesus for one,' I replied.

'At that very moment this cat came flying through the air and landed on the lawn, and he's stayed with us ever since.'

> **'Loving kitten desires position as companion to child.**
> **In exchange will do some light mouse work.'**

Up in heaven, God had just made all the animals and they held a raffle to see who would get what. So the lion got a mane and the leopard got spots and the cat got a meow and things like that. Then at the end, God came down and all the animals lined up to shake his hand. God said, 'Where's the camel?' And St. Peter said, 'The camel's not coming, he's got the hump!'

> A man breaks into a house at night. His is crossing a room when he hears a voice say, 'Jesus and I can see you'.
> He turns round and sees a parrot.
> He says to the parrot, 'You're a clever bird'.
> 'I know.'
> 'What's your name?'
> 'Marmaduke'.
> 'That's a funny name to give a parrot.'
> 'Not as funny as giving the name Jesus to a Rottweiler!'

Sitting with her cat, an old woman was polishing a dusty lamp she had found in the attic, when a genie popped out and offered her three wishes.

Thinking quickly, she said, 'I'd like to be rich. I'd like to be young and I'd like my cat to turn into a handsome prince.'

There was a puff of smoke and the woman found herself young and surrounded by riches. The cat had gone and a gorgeous prince stood beside her, holding out his arms. She melted into his embrace.

'Now,' he whispered, 'aren't you sorry you had me neutered?'

Q. What animal has two humps and is found at the North Pole?
A. A lost camel.

What do you call a camel with no humps?
Humphrey.

A hen and a pig were so fond of their farmer that one day they were discussing how they might please him.

'We could give him a bacon and egg breakfast,' suggested the hen.

'Hold on a bit,' said the pig, 'with you it's an egg, for me it's total commitment.

A man went to a pet shop asking for a canary that sang beautifully. The shopkeeper found one that sang so sweetly it brought tears to the eyes. The customer was just about to buy it when he noticed the bird had only one leg.

'Oh dear', he said. 'That bird only has one leg'.

The shopkeeper replied, 'Look mate, are you looking for a singer or a dancer?'

Two explorers were on a jungle safari when suddenly a ferocious lion jumped in front of them.

'Keep calm, the first explorer whispered. 'Remember what we read in the book about wild animals? If you stand perfectly still and look the lion in the eye, he will turn and run.'

'I know,' replied his companion. 'You've read the book and I've read the book. But has the lion read the book?'

Creeds

I believe in a colour blind God,
Maker of Technicolour people.
Who created the universe
And provided abundant resources
For equitable distribution among all his people.
I believe in Jesus Christ,
Born of a common woman,
Who was ridiculed, disfigured and executed.
Who on the third day rose and fought back;
He storms the highest councils of men
Where he overturns the iron rule of injustice.
From henceforth he shall continue
To judge the hatred and arrogance of men.
I believe in the Spirit of Reconciliation,
The united body of the dispossessed;
The communion of the suffering masses,
The power that overcomes the dehumanising forces of men
The resurrection of personhood, justice and equality.
And in the final triumph of Brotherhood.

Canaan Banana
Zimbabwe

Definitions

Politician: One who approaches every question with an open mouth
Adlai Stevenson

or

...An animal which can sit on a fence and yet keep both ears to the ground
H.L. Mencken

Radical: One with both feet planted firmly in the air
Ranklin D. Roosevelt

A fanatic is someone who can't change his mind and won't change the subject.

On the other hand...
God finds it easier to cool down a fanatic than to warm up a corpse.

Acquaintance: A person whom we know well enough to borrow from but not well enough to lend to.

Atheist: One who has no invisible means of support.

'Is that a mirage over there,' said Paddy, 'or am I seeing things?'

Custard Christains are those people upset by trifles

What do you call parrots' food? POLLYFILLA.

Conscience:
The inner voice which warns us that someone might be looking.

The Arab who invented flavoured crisps was called Sultan Vinegar.

Dentists & Doctors

A letter form a dentist about a regular dental check-up was headed:
'It's time for your 6,000 smile service.'

Man reading his dentist's bill: 'Root canal? He charged me for the Suez Canal'.

Q. What's a dentist's favourite bible verse?
A. '...open thy mouth wide and I shall fill it.'
(Psalm 81 v 11)

Doctor: 'All you need is a rest'
Vicar: 'But, Doctor, look at my tongue'
Doctor: 'Yes, that needs a rest too'

'Where are you going?' asked George.
'To the doctor's' replied Fred, 'I don't like the look of my wife.'
'I'll come with you,' said George, 'I don't like the look of mine either.'

A doctor's receptionist was amazed when a nun slapped the doctors' face and stormed out of the surgery.
'Good gracious,' she said to the doctor, 'What happened?'
'I examined her,' he said, 'and told her she was pregnant.'
'Pregnant? surely not?'
'Of course not,' said the doctor, 'but it cured her hiccups.'

'I'd like my sexual potency lowered', said the old man to the doctor.
'Lowered? It's all in your mind', said the doctor.
'Exactly', said the old man, 'I want it lowered.'

Drivers

One Sunday, shortly after receiving a provisional driving licence, a man drove his parents to church. After a long, rough ride they reached their destination. The man stopped at the entrance to drop his mother off, and when she got out of the car she said, 'Thank you!'
'Any Time' the man replied.
As she slammed the door, the man heard her say, 'I was talking to God!'

Bill hammered on Fred's door and gasped. 'I've just seen somebody stealing your car, but don't worry I've got the number!'

A man was knocked down by a hit-and-run driver.
'Did you get his number?' People asked.
'No', he replied, 'but I'd recognise that laugh anywhere.'

'Waterloo, please,' said the city gent as he jumped into a taxi.
'Is it the station you want?' asked the driver.
'Yes,' the man replied, 'I'm too late for the battle, aren't I?'

Easter

'This being Easter Sunday, we will ask Mrs Brown to come forward and lay an egg on the altar.'

You're Just in Time for Evensong

41

Eating Out

Two nuns sat down in the restaurant: the waitress asked, 'And what is your order? (meaning religious community). 'Egg and chips twice,' came the reply.

A Parson was staying at a Yorkshire country cottage and at breakfast was delighted to hear the lady of the house singing, 'Nearer my God to Thee'. He complimented her on her singing and she replied, 'It's a hymn I boil eggs to—one verse for soft, two for hard.'

'Waiter, waiter, this stew isn't fit for a pig.'
'I'll take it away, sir, and bring you some that is.'

'Waiter, waiter, is there rice pudding on the menu?'
'There was sir, but I've wiped it off.'

Environment

On a can of room freshener: 'Bring the clean, natural freshness of a country meadow indoors. Freshens the air in your home with a clean, back-to-nature scent—as refreshing as the summer grass and fragrant flowers of a country meadow.
'WARNING: inhaling the contents can be harmful or fatal.'

**A minister was addressing the local children in a sermon on 'honesty.' 'Suppose you were walking along the street behind me,' he said, 'and I dropped a £10 note.
What would you do?'
An eager hand shot up.
'Pick it up and put it in the litter bin.'**

Epitaphs

Here lies a poor woman who was always tired,
Who lived in a house where help was not hired.
Her last words on earth, 'Dear Friends I am going where washing ain't
done, nor sweeping or sewing.

But everything there is exact to my wishes. For there they don't eat,
there's no washing of dishes.

I'll be where loud anthems will always be ringing. But having no voice
I'll get clear of the singing.

Don't mourn for me now or ever, I am going to do nothing, for ever
and ever.'

Poster in a cemetery: WAKE UP YOUR COUNTRY NEEDS YOU!

**And from a tombstone
in Australia...**

R . I . P .

I TOLD YOU I WAS ILL.

Spike Milligan's epitaph
I DEMAND A SECOND OPINION

She lived with her husband for 50 years.
She died in the confident hope of a better life.

A devout Yorkshire Methodist lady died and her husband pondered over a
suitable epitaph for her headstone.
He settled for—'She was thine'.
When he went to see it, he was upset to see they had carved 'She was thin'.
'You've missed the 'e' off', he said.
'Don't worry' they said, come back in half-an-hour. We'll put the 'e' in.'
Half-an-hour later he read, 'E She was thin!'

Europe

'I am sure Synod members will know that wicked description of a European hell where the Germans are the police; the Swedes are the comedians; the Italians are the army; Frenchmen dig the road; Belgians are the pop singers; the Spaniards run the railways; Turks cook the food; the Irish are waiters; the clergy are Welsh; Scots run the bars; Greeks run the government and the common language is Dutch. A peculiar refinement for the English is that we think we are paying for it all'.

Quotation by The Archbishop of York. John Habjood, during a General Synod.

Isn't this European thing getting out of hand, Ponsonby?

Lech Walesa's regal aspirations led to a new cottage industry in Poland: Walesa jokes. One story has it that the electrician and presidential candidate is musing on the question of where he should be buried.

Initially, he settles on Wawel Cathedral in Krakow, where most of Poland's kings have been laid to rest. Becoming dissatisfied with this idea, he plumps instead for the Vatican, surely a more appropriate place for a good Catholic of his stature.

Finally, he decides to be buried in Jerusalem, near the Holy Sepulchre. He asks the Israeli authorities whether such a burial can be arranged. Yes, he is told, for a price: £25,000.

'£25,000', said Walesa, 'that's ridiculous for just three days!'

After the break Jason sneaked an ice lolly into the geography class. He had just got seated when the teacher asked, 'Jason, what do we call people who live in Europe?'
'Don't know miss,' he said.
'European!' shouted a voice from the back.
'No, I'm not', said Jason indignently. 'My ice lolly's melting!'

Isn't It Great to be British

Ee, isn't it great to be British?
It fills me with infinite pride,
What can compare
With that spirit so rare?
The old bulldog is there by my side.

Yet the shoes that I wear are Italian,
My tie was fashioned in France,
My shirts are too long
They were made in Hong Kong,
I can tell that with simply a glance.

It's a Japanese car that I'm driving,
It's a Taiwan transistor I hear,
My video set is Norwegian,
Yet it fills me with comfort and cheer.

My fridge is a product of Holland,
My washing machine made in Spain,
My sun lamp equipment
Is part of a shipment
From Sweden
Its heat helps the pain.

Oh isn't it fun to be British?
To be brave, to be strong, to be free.
Yet on looking around
The truth is, I found,
The only thing British—is me!

Farming

**A sign supposedly seen on a farm gate:
'Trespassers may enter free. The bull will charge later.'**

Farmer Jones heard that if you played music to cows they produced more milk.
Well, lo and behold, when he played Brahm's Lullaby he got two buckets from
each cow.
When he played 'Rock around the clock' he got four buckets per cow!
Then he played, 'The flight of the bumblebee' and had to swim for his life!

*A vicar walking in the country with his wife had forgotten his watch, so when he saw a
farmer milking a cow he shouted, 'can you tell me the time?'*
The farmer slowly lifted the cow's udders and replied, 'two thirty'.
'That's amazing', said the vicar, you can tell the time from the cow's udders?'
'No', said the farmer, 'if I lift them up high enough, I can just see the village clock!'

Funerals

The Welsh like to add a person's occupation to his name—Dai the Coal
or Will the Fish, for example. In one small town were two Ernies, one a
travel agent and one an undertaker. They were known as Ernie the
Journey and Ernie the Final Journey.

During a period when industrial
unrest threatened the smooth running of funerals in the cemetery
normally used for Christian burials in
Bombay, the lady in charge, a Miss
Dyer (!) sent out the following memo:
'During the period of the strike, the
cemetery will be operated by a
skeleton staff.'

*A minister was conducting the
funeral service of one of his congregation. He spoke so highly of
the man's virtues and went on
about how respected and admired
he had been, that the widow
leaned over and whispered to her
son, 'We'd better get out of here,
I think we've come to the wrong
funeral.'*

Garages

'I'm afraid, brother, that you have left undone those things
which you ought to have done!'

Gardening

Plant four rows of peas:

Preparedness
Promptness
Perseverance and
Prayer.

Then plant three rows of squash:

Squash gossip
Squash criticism
Squash indifference.

Add five rows of lettuce:

Let us be faithful
Let us be unselfish
Let us be loyal
Let us be truthful and
let us love one another.

But no garden is complete without turnips:

Turn up to meetings
Turn up with a smile
Turn up new ideas
Turn up with real determination.

A young boy was helping his grandfather lift potatoes.
After a while the child began to tire.
'Grandpa,' he asked wearily, 'what made you bury these things anyway?'

Grandparents

A grandmother is a lady who has no children of her own, so she likes other people's kids. A grandfather is a man grandmother. He likes to go on walks with the kids and they talk about fishing and things like that.

Grandmas don't have to do anything except be there. They're old, so they shouldn't play hard or run. They let us ride the 'pretend horse' at the supermarket and have plenty of 20p's ready. They take us on slow walks and always stop for things like caterpillars and pretty leaves. They never say 'Hurry up'.

Usually they are fat, but not too fat to tie kids' shoes. They wear glasses and funny underwear. They don't have to be smart, only answer questions like, 'Why do dogs hate cats?' and 'Why isn't God married?'

Everybody should try to have one, because grandmas and grandpas are the only grownups who have got time.

Grandma were you in the Ark?

No I wasn't!

Then how come you weren't drowned?

Grandfather Jones was quite deaf but although he couldn't hear the sermon he went to Church every Sunday.
'Why do you go to Church when you can't hear what's going on?' asked one of his grandchildren.
Grandfather considered for a moment and then said,
'I want everyone to know whose side I'm on.'

Growing Old

There is a danger that when you are old, your illness is thought to be because you are old. Alex Comfort has a wonderful story about a gentleman of 104 who complained of an awful pain in his leg. The doctor said: 'Well, what can you expect at your age?' The man replied, 'My other leg is 104 and that hasn't got a pain.'

George Burns speaking on his television special, 'George Burns' 95th Birthday Party': 'People are always asking me when I'm going to retire. Why should I? I've got the best of both worlds—I'm still making films and I'm a senior citizen so I can see myself for half price.'

'What are seniors worth?—Remember, old folks are worth a fortune—with silver in their hair, gold in their teeth, stones in their kidneys, lead in their feet and gas in their stomachs!'

A Senior Citizen is one who was here before the pill, television, frozen food, credit cards and ball point pens.
For us, time-sharing meant togetherness, not computers, and a chip meant a piece of wood or a piece of fried potato. Hardware meant durable—and software did not exist as a word.
Porn meant going to 'Uncles' for a loan and teenagers never wore jeans. We were before panti-hose, drip-dry, dishwashers, tumble-driers and the electric blanket.
We got married first and then lived together (how quaint can one be?) Girls wore Peter Pan collars and thought cleavage was something the butcher did.
We were before Batman, vitamin pills, disposable nappies, pizzas, instant coffee and Chinese takeaways. '
In our day cigarette smoking was fashionable, grass was for mowing, pot was a cooking utensil and a gay person was the 'life and soul of the party' and nothing more, whilst aids meant just beauty treatment or help for someone in trouble.
We senior citizens must be a hardy bunch when you think of the way in which the world has changed and the adjustments we have had to survive.

'Frankly, I have become a frivolous old girl. I wake up with five gentlemen each day. Will Power helps me out of bed. Then next I go to see John. Arthur Ritis shows up about this time and stays the rest of the day. He doesn't like to stay in one place very long, so he takes me from joint to joint. After such a busy day I'm really tired and glad to go to bed with Johnnie Walker. Recently I've also been flirting with Al Zymer!'

Retirement is twice as much husband and half as much money.

How Do You Know You Are Growing Old?

Everything hurts—what doesn't hurt, doesn't work,
The gleam in your eye is the sun glinting on your bi-focals.
You feel like the morning after, but you haven't been anywhere.
You get winded playing cards.
Your children begin to look middle-aged.
You join a health club but don't go.
You know all the answers but nobody asks the questions.
You look forward to a dull evening.
You need glasses to find your glasses.
You turn out the light for economy, instead of romance.
You sit in the rocking chair but can't make it go.
Your knees buckle but your belt won't.
Your back goes out more than you do.
Your house is too big and your medicine chest not big enough.
You sink your teeth into a steak and they stay there.
Your birthday cake collapses under the weight of the candles.

Even people are changing; they are so much younger than they used to be when I was their age. On the other hand people my own age are so much older than I am. I ran into an old friend the other day and she had aged so much that she did not recognise me.

I got to thinking about the poor thing whilst I was combing my hair this morning, and while I was doing that I glanced at my reflection—and do you know what? They don't make mirrors like they used to.

Three old men lived in a house together. One day, Fred ran the bath and when he had one foot in, he couldn't remember whether he was half way in or half way out.
'Bill', shouted Fred, 'Am I getting in this bath or out?'
'Hold on ', said Bill, 'I'm coming up the stairs'.
Half way up, he shouted, 'Charlie! Am I going up stairs or down?'
'I'm fed up with you two', shouted Charlie, 'you're both as thick as this table.' He knocked hard on the table, then said— 'Is that somebody at the back door or the front?'

Harvest

The Sunday School children were in the church at the beginning of a Harvest Thanksgiving service. When they went into their schoolroom they were asked what they had seen in the church. There were quick replies of potatoes, cabbages, onions, peas, beans etc. Then the teacher asked: 'Can you give me a name that would cover all those?' After a pause and much thought, the answer from a small boy was...'Gravy, Miss.'

HARVEST FESTIVAL

Perhaps that lump of cheddar wasn't such a good idea!

A Methodist Church was looking for a special preacher for a Harvest Festival. The secretary contacted the theological college and asked if they could send a student, preferably one who was a wit. On the given day two students arrived with a note from the principal. 'Sorry, we're a bit short on wits. Have sent two half-wits instead.'

The vicar placed a notice on the Vicarage Orchard which said, 'Please do not take these apples and pears—they are needed for the harvest festival. But the fruit disappeared and an additional notice read.
'All is safely gathered in'.

Heaven and Hell

I dreamt Death came the other night
And Heaven's Gate swung wide,
An Angel, with a halo bright,
Ushered me inside.
And there to my astonishment
Were folks I'd judged and labelled.
As 'Quite unfit' 'Of little worth'
And 'Spiritually disabled'.
Indignant words rose to my lips
But never were set free
For every face showed stunned surprise,
No one expected me.

When the gate between Heaven and Hell needed mending, St Peter told the Devil it was his responsibility to have it repaired. But he declined. So Peter got tough and declared 'I'll sue you.'
Knowing this to be a bluff, Old Nick replied: 'Oh yeah, and where are you going to find a lawyer?'

A mischievous boy was asked by his mother, 'How do you expect to get to heaven?'
He thought for a moment and said, 'Well I shall just run in and out and keep slamming the door until they say "For goodness sake come in or stay out", and I'll go in.'

Talking of Heaven, a parachutist was hurtling towards earth when his parachute failed to open. As he plummeted downward he passed a bloke going upwards at speed.
'Know anything about parachutes?' he cried.
'Not a lot,' he replied. 'Do you know anything about gas ovens!'

And still talking about Heaven: a vicar caught some children throwing stones at the church windows.
'Behave yourselves,' he cried, 'don't you want to go to Heaven?'
'Yes,' said one chastened youngster.
'No,' said another.
'No! Don't you want to go to Heaven when you die?' asked the vicar.
'Oh! When I die?' said the boy, 'I thought you were getting a trip up now!'

When a man approached the gates of Heaven and asked to be let in,
St Peter said to him, 'Tell me one good thing you did in your life.'
'Well,' replied the fellow, 'I saw a group of thugs harassing an elderly woman, so I kicked their leader in the shins.'
'When did this happen?'
'About 40 seconds ago.'

Holy Days and Holidays

An aeroplane flew into turbulent weather. To keep the passengers calm, the flight attendants wheeled out the drinks trolley.

'I'd like a mineral water,' said a woman in the first row. Moving along, the stewardess asked the man behind her if he would like something.

'Yes, please,' he replied. 'Just give me whatever the pilot is drinking.'

A parishioner returned home from his holidays with a bottle of cherry brandy. Knowing that the minister was partial to cherry brandy, despite some of his flock being strictly teetotal, he gave it to him on the understanding that the minister would acknowledge the gift in the following month's church magazine. The following notice duly appeared: 'The minister wishes to thank Mr Smith for his gift of fruit—and the spirit in which it was given.'

'Having recently returned from their visit to Mexico, the Smith's discussed their trip and showed their slides, which made us all want to leave immediately.'

Notice in a Majorcan hotel bedroom:
'Guests do not have to get themselves hot in this room.
Please control yourselves.'

The British airline captain grew more frustrated as his departure was repeatedly put back. When he was finally about to move, a German airliner was given immediate clearance instead.

Calling up Ground Control he demanded to know why another aircraft had been given the slot. Before they could answer, the German captain cut in: 'Because we get up very early and leave our towels on the end of the runway.'

Hospital

The outspoken vicar of a country parish was rushed to hospital for an emergency appendix operation. The chairman of the parish council visited him as he was recovering and said, 'At our meeting last night I proposed we send you a get well soon message, and I am pleased to say it was passed by nine votes to eight.

> Sign spotted in a clinic:
> 'Despite the increase in the cost of living the demand for it continues.'

Howlers!

- *Adolescence is the stage between puberty and adultery.*
- *Karl Marx was one of the Marx Brothers.*
- *People who live in Moscow are called Mosquitoes.*

The Romans made their roads straight so that the Britons could not hide round the corners.

Queen Elizabeth had a difficult reign because Mary Queen of Scots was always hoovering in the background.

> **From an essay:**
> 'Vesuvius is a volcano. You can climb to the top, look over the rim and see the Creator smoking!'

'Noah's wife was called Joan of Arc'

'When Mary heard she was to be the mother of Jesus she went off and sang the Magna Carta'

'Paraffin is next in order after Seraphim'.

CITY LIBRARY

THE HOLY BIBLE

DOGMA

Henry VIII thought so much of Wolsey that he made him a cardigan

The Fifth Commandment is: Humour Thy father and mother

A deacon is a mass of flammable material

Lot's wife was a pillar of salt by day...and a ball of fire by night

Salome was a woman who danced naked in front of Harrods

Holy acrimony is another name for marriage

Christians each have only one wife. This is called monotony

The Pope lives in a vacuum

Today wild beasts are confined to Theological Gardens

The patron saint of travellers is called St Francis of the seasick

It is sometimes difficult to hear what is being said in church because the agnostics are so terrible

Arabs wear turbines on their heads.

Sir Francis Drake circumcised the globe with a 100 foot clipper.

Three kinds of blood vessels are arteries, veins and caterpillars.

A navigator is the strap which a navvy wears under his knees to stop rats running up his leg

The appendix is part of a book for which no-one has yet discovered a use

Massacre is black stuff people put on their eyes

I must draw a one inch virgin on the left hand side of each page

Hamlet—a little eggs beaten up with some bacon

Insurance

AA bosses say the excuses given by motorists for accidents have never been so inventive. Here are examples from AA files:

- 'The pedestrian had no idea which direction to run, so I ran over him.'
- 'Coming home, I drove into the wrong house and collided with a tree I don't have.'
- 'I saw a slow-moving, sad-faced old gentleman as he bounced off the roof of my car.'
- 'I collided with a stationary truck coming the other way.'
- 'I thought my window was down, but I found out it was up when I put my head through it.'
- 'The guy was all over the road. I had to swerve a number of times before I hit him.'
- 'I pulled away from the side of the road, glanced at my mother-in-law and headed over the embankment.'

- 'I told the police I was not injured, but on removing my hat I found I had a fractured skull.'

Jesus

There is but one Lord Jesus and one faith, and the rest is a dispute about trifles.

Queen Elizabeth I

> *Had the doctrines of Jesus been preached always as pure as they came from his lips, the whole civilised world would now have been Christian.*
>
> Thomas Jefferson

Found at the Union Theological Seminary, New York: Jesus said to them, 'Who do you say that I am?' And they replied, 'You are the eschatological manifestation of the ground of our being, the Kerygma, in which we find the ultimate meaning of our inter-personal relationships.' And Jesus said, 'Yer what?'

Jews

One of the attractive features of Jewish life is that, despite the heartaches, they can still laugh at themselves.

Hami had died so his widow went to the local ads office to put the announcement in the paper—
'Hami Dead'.
'You are allowed three more words for your £3 madam.' said the sales girl.
'Really?' said Hami's widow. After some thought she added—
Hami dead. Volvo for sale.

When Groucho Marx was told that he was not allowed to swim at the country club because he was Jewish, he asked, 'And what about my son—he's only half Jewish, can he go in up to his waist?'

'Even Moses couldn't get along with the Jews.'
(Yiddish Proverb)

Israel's veteran politician, Dr Yosef Burg, is the master of the verbal nicety. His telegram to the Chief Rabbi, Immanuel Jakobovits, congratulating him on his peerage read simply: 'Our shepherd is a Lord.'

Jewish Chronicle

A Jewish mother pestered a famous conductor to give her boy a chance to play the violin for him. 'He is brilliant', she pleaded, 'just listen to this tape.' Soon the beautiful sounds of Bruch's violin concerto filled the room and the conductor's eyes filled with tears.
'Is that your boy?' he asked.
'No', she said. 'that's Jascha Heifetz, but my boy plays just like him.'

A Jew owns a remarkable parrot—it can 'daven' (pray in Hebrew).
He decides to take it to the synagogue and make some money. After the
service he gathers 20 or so acquaintances round him.
'This parrot' he announces 'can daven'
'Psha! Piffle!' they all cry.
'OK, so we'll take a bet'
Odds of 25-to-one-against are agreed, the money is laid on the table.
'OK, go ahead' he instructs the parrot.
The parrot does not move.
'Go on, daven'
Nothing.
He cajoles and begs the parrot to daven, but to no avail.
He pays out a fortune.
When he gets the parrot home he is about to strangle it, when the bird says,
'Wait! Wait! See what odds you get next week!'

After the six day war in Israel, Golda Meir became
Prime Minster of Israel and Richard Nixon became
President of the USA. When they met Nixon was
effusive in his praise of Israel's military prowess.
'Incredible', he said, 'winning a war in six days.
I would like to meet your generals.'
'Right', said Golda Meir, we'll send Levi Eshkol and
Moshe Dayan
but we want two of your generals to come to Israel.'
'Who do you want?' asked the President.
After a pause Golda Meir said, 'General Motors and
General Electric!'

Love and Marriage

A couple whose passion had waned consulted a marriage guidance counsellor. Several sessions later, after little success, the counsellor swept the woman into his arms and kissed her.

'You see,' he said to the husband, 'this is the sort of treatment your wife needs—every Monday, Thursday and Saturday, at least.'

'Well,' replied the husband, 'I can bring her here on Thursdays and Saturdays, but Monday is my bowling night.'

Grainews

A middle aged couple were married during the week. After the wedding the groom asked the minister, 'How much do I owe you?'
The minister said, 'How much is she worth?'
The groom gave the minister £1. The minister took a second look at the bride and gave him 50p back.

'One reason why it's hard to save money,' the housewife complained, 'is that our neighbours are always buying something we can't afford.'

A farmer one evening saw a light moving across the farmyard. He found, on investigation that it was his hired man, who was dressed up and carrying a lantern. On being asked where he was going with the lantern, the man replied, 'Ah'm off courtin'.

'Courtin?' queried the farmer. 'Ah nivver took a lantern when ah went courtin.'

'Naw,' said the man, 'Ah thowt not when ah saw thi missus.'

Walking in the park one day, a couple noticed a young man and woman sitting on a bench, kissing passionately.

'Why don't you do that?' complained the wife.

'But darling,' replied the husband, 'I don't even know the woman.'

Do you think we should ban confetti in future?

'When I asked you to talk to me more, I didn't mean during Coronation Street!'

A husband and wife drove for miles in silence after an argument in which neither would budge. The husband pointed to a mule in a paddock, 'Relative of yours?' he asked.
'Yes,' said the wife, 'by marriage.'

Conversation between man and wife:
'According to the Guinness Book of Records, a Russian woman produced sixty-nine children.'
'Sixty-nine kids! That's hard to believe.'
'I wonder why she didn't go for a round seventy!'
'Who knows? Maybe she wanted a career, too.'

A young chap asked his prospective father-in-law for his daughter's hand in marriage.
'Have you seen her mother?' the father asked.
'Yes' the lad replied, 'but I still prefer your daughter'.

Signing the register at a wedding, the best man had difficulty making his ball point pen work. 'Put your weight on it', said the Vicar. He duly signed: 'John Smith (10 stone 14 pound)!'

She took him for better or worse, but he was worse than she took him for.

Heard in the village shop: 'Have you got one of them blank cards for birthdays? It's my husbands tomorrow but we're not speaking at the moment.'

Management Consultants

From:
Jordan Management Consultants,
Jerusalem

To:
Jesus,
Son of Joseph,
Carpenter's Shop,
Nazareth

It is our opinion that the twelve men you have picked to manage your new organisation lack the background, educational and vocational aptitude for the type of enterprise you are undertaking. They do not have the team concept.

Simon Peter is emotionally unstable and given to fits of temper. Andrew has no qualities of leadership. The two brothers James and John place personal interest above company loyalty. Thomas demonstrates a questioning attitude that would tend to undermine morale.

We feel it is our duty to tell you that Matthew has been blacklisted by the Greater Jerusalem Better Business Bureau. James the son of Alphaeus, and Thaddaeus have radical leanings, and both registered high on the manic-depressive scale.

One of the candidates, however, shows great potential. His is a man of ability and resourcefulness, has a keen business mind and contacts in high places. He is highly motivated and ambitious. We recommend Judas Iscariot as your controller and right-hand man.

We wish you every success in your new venture.

Yours faithfully

Mistaken Impressions

A young couple about to be married were looking at a house in the country and after satisfying themselves that it was suitable they started home. During the trip home the young lady was very thoughtful and when asked why, she replied, 'Did you notice any W.C.? (meaning water closet). The young man replied to the effect that he had not noticed any, whereupon he wrote to the owner to find out where it was located. The owner did not understand the meaning of W.C. but finally concluded that it meant 'Wesleyan Chapel' and answered as follows:

Dear Sir,

Have great pleasure in informing you that the WC is situated nine miles from the house and is capable of seating 200 people.

This is an important situation if you are in the habit of going regularly, but no doubt you will be glad to know that many people who go there take their lunch with them and make a day of it, while others who cannot spare the time go by car.

You might be interested to know that my daughter was married in the WC. In fact, it was there that she met her husband.

I remember the marriage well on account of the rush for seats.

There were ten people on a seat usually occupied by two, and it was wonderful to watch the expression on their faces.

My brother was there, he has gone regularly since the day he was christened.

Residents erected a bell over the WC to be rung each time a member enters.

A Bazaar is to be held, the proceeds to help provide plush seats, as members think this is a long felt need.

My wife and I do not go as much as we should do.

It is six years since we last went and I can assure you it pains us both very much not being able to go more often.

Little Misunderstandings

Children have keen hearing but limited experience. Adults do not always articulate clearly. So we shouldn't be surprised to learn that one child felt secure in the knowledge that: 'Surely good Mrs Murphy shall follow me all the days of my life,' and that another visualised a school in which 'Christ the Royal Master leans against the phone.'

Money

Give and Take
One of the funny things about the stock market
is that every time one person buys, another
sells, and they both think they are astute.

> Sad was the young man whose
> girlfriend refused to marry him for
> religious reasons. He was broke, and
> she worshipped money.

Mums and Dads

Teenager to friend: 'My mother put on weight
because of shame—it's a shame to waste the rest
of this, it's a shame to waste the rest of that.'

Three little boys were discussing what their fathers did.
The first one said, 'My father puts together a few
words, calls it poetry and gets £20 for it.'
The second one said, 'My father puts together a few
pieces of wood, calls it sculpture and gets £50 for it.'
'That's nothing,' said the third boy, 'My father writes a
few notes, calls it a sermon and it takes four men to
carry the money.'

My Mean Mother

I had the meanest Mother in the world.

While other kids had lollies for breakfast, I had to eat cereal, egg and toast. While other kids had cans of drinks and lollies for lunch, I had to have a sandwich. As you can guess, my dinner was different from other kids too...as well as the food, we had to eat at a table and not in front of the television.

My mother also insisted on knowing where we were at all times. She had to know who our friends were, where we were going and even told us what time we had to be home.

You'd think we were on a chain gang or something.

I am ashamed to admit it, but my Mother had the nerve to break child labour laws. She made us work, we had to wash dishes, make our beds and even learn to cook. That woman must have stayed awake at nights just thinking up things for us kids to do.

She always insisted that we tell the truth, the whole truth and nothing but the truth.

By the time we were teenagers, our whole life became more unbearable. No tooting the car horn for the girls in our family to come running. She embarrassed us by insisting that the boys came to the door to get us.

I forgot to mention that most of our friends were allowed to date at the mature age of 12 or 13. Our old-fashioned Mother refused to let us date before we were at least 15.

She really raised a bunch of squares. None of us kids were arrested for shoplifting or busted for dope.

And who do you think we have to thank for that?

You're right...our mean Mother.

Every day we hear cries from both our people and politicians about what our country really needs.

What our country really needs is more mean Mothers like mine.

Newspaper Reports

Sentences that could have been better constructed include the report of a visit to Walsingham:

'Afterwards the Bishop walked among the crowds, eating their picnic lunches'.

A song festival was hell at the Methodist Church

Amongst letters of complaint received by the editor of a local weekly newspaper were the following:

'You impaired my reputation by reporting that my lecture about Saturn was about Satan, especially as you said it was illustrated with slides I took in the vicarage garden.'

'I trust that there were no hidden motives behind your report that our Legion fete was held in a shady Alderman's garden'. Ald. Wiggesworth proudly bears an unblemished reputation.'

Christians living in Reading who happened to browse through the sports pages of their local paper must have been startled by one particular headline. A story of Reading Cricket Club's defeat in the semi-final of the William Younger Cup was headed: 'Reading miss out on Lord's return?'

In a Local Newspaper—An account of a Church gathering
The sudden gust of wind took all at the ceremony by surprise. Hats were blown off and copies of the minister's sermon and other rubbish were scattered over the site.

These headlines have appeared in English-language newspapers around the world:

- 20 year friendship ends at the altar
- 'Fidelio' only opera Beethoven wrote on Monday evening
- Prisoners escape after execution
- Sisters wed brothers have babies same day
- Passengers hit by cancelled trains

Our magazine editor works for the Sun.

Noah

I don't know what it is about Noah that makes him an ideal subject for humorous verse but he certainly inspires plenty. Here are two examples:

The Lord Said Unto Noah

The Lord said unto Noah
'Where is the Ark I commanded you to build?'
And Noah said
'Verily, I have had three carpenters off sick,
The Gopher wood supplier has let me down,
Yea, even though the Gopher wood hath been
  on order for nigh upon twelve months and
The damp course specialist hath not turned up.'
God said to Noah
'I want the Ark finished before seven days and seven nights'
Noah said
'It will be so.'
But it was not so.
The Lord said unto Noah
'What seems to be the trouble this time?'
Noah said
'My subcontractor hath gone bankrupt,
The pitch for the outside of the Ark hath not arrived,
The glazier departeth on holiday to Majorca,
Yea, even though I offered him double time!
Shem hath formed a pop group with his brothers
Ham and Japheth—Lord I am undone.'
The Lord grew angry and said
'What about the animals? Two of every sort I have ordered to be
  kept alive. Where, for example, are the giraffes?'
And Noah said
'They hath been delivered to the wrong address but should arrive by Friday'
And the Lord said unto Noah
'Where are the monkeys and the elephants and the zebras?'
Noah said
'They are expected today'
The Lord said
'How about the unicorns?'
And Noah wrung his hands and wept
'Oh Lord—they are a discontinued line—Thou can'st not get
  unicorns for love nor money. Thou knowest how it is'
And the Lord said
'Noah my son, I know—why else doest thou think I have caused the flood.
             Anonymous

Flood

The teacher in a junior school, said, 'Sit in a circle round me,
I'll tell you a story about a big ship, that never went near to the sea!'
The children, who obeyed their elders, sat in the way they were told
And listened with awe as this story, of a ship, by the teacher, was told.
'God came', said the teacher, 'from Yorkshire, like Noah and his family, too.
In a dream, God said, to old Noah, 'Here's what I want thee to do;
Get thee some wood and some rivets and build thee a massive big boat,
It must be a long and wide 'un, above all, I want it to float'.
So Noah chopped wood and made rivets, his arms ached and nearly fell off,
He didn't have time to be poorly, not even to sneeze or to cough,
The wood that he used was called Gopher, water-proofed over with pitch,
Noah's wife also was busy, she'd hundreds of curtains to stitch!
Noah worked hard at his labours and when he had done the assembly,
The boat was a hundred and fifty yards long, that's thirty yards longer than
      Wembley.
Noah was nearly six hundred years old, his strength was beginning to fail,
God, feeling sorry for Noah, poor man, said, 'Don't build a mast nor a sail.
Tha's made a good job out of building thi boat, tha's built it high, wi three decks,
There isn't much more for thee Noah, to do, here's what tha's got to do next.
All t'living things as is on this earth, tha gathers a lad and a lass,
And when tha has done it—and I'm watching thee—summat is coming to pass.
Now listen, old Noah, to what I've to say, it's me as thart going to please,
So get two on everything as tha can find, from elephants, reight down to fleas!'
Well, Noah, his sons and his grandsons, were busy from daylight to dark,
One night, God said, 'I've been thinking, this boat, we shall call it an Ark'.
They gathered up thousands of creatures, two of each sort they could find;
Till the Ark was filled, nearly bursting, yet millions they had left behind!
God looked and smiled on old Noah, said, 'Eeh, thart doing alreight,
Naa go and get thee some fodder, tha'll all want summat to eight.
There's one more thing I've to tell thee, get watter-proof shoes for thi feet,
When thee and thi family are sleeping, it's going to start raining, toneet!'
God kept the promise to Noah he'd made, that night, it started to rain,
The land was flooded, a million feet deep (they hadn't invented the drain).
For forty days and forty nights, it rained through dark and light,
Until at last, the mountain tops were hidden from their sight.
It was a long time until it eased off, falling from the skies,
One month, one week and three days it took, if you must be precise,
Their troubles were not over yet, though, despite all the time that had passed,
Another half year had to go by, plus fifty more days till at last,
Two hundred and thirty days total, from the time it had started to rain,
Would pass, till the Ark of old Noah, ever felt dry land again!
It happened to rest on a mountain, the highest there was round about,
So Noah, he sent off a raven, to do what you might have called scout.
The raven returned empty handed, or would you prefer empty claws?

The reason he came back with nothing, was purely and simply because
All other mountains there were in the world, were still covered deep by the rain,
Eighty more days would have to pass by, before they were dry land again!
Ten months from the night it had started to rain, God looked down from above,
Commanded the waters should subside again, and Noah, he sent out a dove.
In a short while, the dove she returned, she carried an Olive Leaf,
Noah knelt down in the Ark and he prayed, unshaken in his belief.
At last, the dove, she flew off again, this time she didn't come back,
Noah went out through a door in the Ark, this time, not wearing a mac.
The waters receded and all Noah's sons, they went and they searched far
     and wide,
Those of his lads who hadn't yet wed, went off in search of a Bride.
Have you any questions?' the young teacher asked, looking around at her band;
One cheeky girl, it seemed had the nerve and slowly she lifted her hand,
'What colour curtains did Noah's wife choose?' a question the teacher thought
     crass,
'You'd better ask Mrs Simpkins', she said, 'she takes the embroidery class!'

Les Hanson

I wish they'd get a spin dryer

**What sort of lighting did Noah have on the ark?
No, not arc lighting—it was flood lighting.**

The most successful businessman the world has ever known was Noah. He floated
a successful company while the rest of the world was going into liquidation.

Notice Boards

On Sunday a special collection will be taken to defray the cost of the new carpet.
All those wishing to do something on the carpet, please come forward and get a piece of paper.

Work for the Lord—the pay isn't much but the retirement plan is out of this world.

Sign outside the Elvin Pentecostal Church, Willesden:
'Try our healing service. You won't get better.'

The notice outside Windsor's Holy Trinity Church read:
'Open legally on Sunday.'
Underneath someone could not resist the temptation of adding:
'From the people who brought you Christmas.'

A passer-by was surprised to see this notice:
St Andrew's Church
THE MESSIAH
Here next Sunday

Appearing on a wayside pulpit alongside a bus stop were the words,
'Where will you be on the day of judgement?'
Underneath someone had written—'Still here, waiting for a No. 57 bus!'

A notice outside Chichester Cathedral advertising lunch time concerts said:
'Sandwiches may be eaten'
someone had scrawled underneath:
'So if you are a sandwich don't come.'

Notice in church hall kitchen:
Ladies when you have emptied the teapot please stand upside down in the sink.
To this has now been added:
No hot bottoms on the Formica.

Those of you who think you know everything
Are annoying to those of us who do!

There is a story attributed to Bernard Manning that he was out walking with a friend in Cambridge when they came upon a wayside pulpit notice which carried the quotation: 'I do not mind where I go as long as it is forward.' The friend went to the notice and wrote underneath, 'And so say all of us signed, The Gadarene Swine.'

Sign outside a church:

Come in and have your faith lifted

Optimists and Pessimists

'Optimists are wrong just as often as pessimists, but they enjoy life!'

'How dismal you look,' observed a bucket to his companion as they were going to the well.
'Ah,' replied the other, 'I was reflecting on the uselessness of our being filled, for though we always go away full, we always come back empty.'
'Dear me, how strange to look at it that way,' said the first bucket.
'I enjoy the thought that however empty we come, we always go away full.'

An optimist is a man who thinks the preacher is nearly through when he says 'Finally...'

Organists

Now that we've overhauled the organ you can change your combinations without taking your feet of the pedals!

A deaf organ blower in a village church always continued to provide wind long after the singing of the hymns had finished. One Sunday, the exasperated organist wrote a note and asked a choirboy to give it to the blower. The choirboy, misunderstanding the organist, delivered the note to the vicar, who was in the pulpit. It read: 'Will you please shut your row. People come here to hear me play, not to listen to your noise.'.

'I am the vicar of this church and I earn £80 per week and it isn't fair.'
'I am the verger at this church and I get £40 per week and it isn't fair.'
'I am the organist at this church and I get £50 per day and there's no business like show business'.

Parent to Teacher

Dear Teacher,

'Last year my son was the hotelier in the nativity play.
Why have you demoted him to a common carpenter this year?'

*I kept Jane at home yesterday because my wife had twins
and I can assure you this will not happen again.*

**Please excuse Moira for not being at school this week.
I have been upside down with the painters for the last 3 days.**

Please excuse Jimmy for being. It was his father's fault.

Please excuse Roy he has loose vowels.

My boy hasn't been to school. He has diarrhoea through a hole in his shoe.

*I am sorry you have branded my son illiterate.
This is a dirty lie as I was married a week before he was born.*

You have changed my little girl into a boy. Will this make any difference?

Parish Magazines

Mr Bradfield was elected and has accepted the office of Churchwarden.
We could not get a better man.

*Some of our friends who make regular subscriptions have died during the
year, but we would like to think that there are others who would consider
doing the same.*
Thank you.

There will be a procession next Sunday afternoon in the grounds
of the Monastery, but if it rains in the afternoon, the procession will
take place in the morning.

*Next Sunday, Mrs Vinsion will be soloist for the morning service.
The rector will then speak on 'it's a terrible experience'.*

The rector spoke briefly, much to the delight of the audience.

The rector will preach his farewell message,
after which the choir will sing, 'Break forth into joy.'

For those of you who have children and don't know it, we have a nursery downstairs.

**During the absence of our rector, we enjoyed the rare
privilege of hearing a good sermon when J.F. Stubbs
supplied our pulpit.**

Police Notices

Thieves stole a van containing bottles of hair restorer.
Police are now combing the area.

Two men robbed a city bank today. One is described as being seven feet tall, the other four foot six inches. Police are looking high and low for them.

Hundreds of stray dogs disappeared yesterday. Police say they have no leads.

A lorry containing onions has shed its load on the motorway. Motorists are advised to find a hard shoulder to cry on!

Two tankers have collided in the channel—one carrying blue paint, the other red. The crews are said to be marooned.

A van loaded with 100s of copies of Roget's Thesaurus collided with a taxi this afternoon. Witnesses were astonished...shocked...caught off guard...surprised...startled... dumfounded and thunderstruck!

Prayers

Tommy and his brother Peter were being put to bed by their Grandma who had come to stay for Christmas. While they were undressing Grandma popped into the bathroom to tidy up after them.
They knelt to say their prayers and Tommy ended up in a loud voice with a request for a pair of roller skates for Christmas.
'Not so loud,' said Peter, God isn't deaf.'
'No, of course not,' replied Tommy, 'but Grandma is.'

The Baptist minister and his wife had been on holiday. At the first prayer meeting held after their return, a good brother got down on his knees, and said: 'Oh Lord, we thank Thee for bringing back our beloved Pastor. We are glad to have him among us once again and we praise Thee that Thou has cared for him and his wife, for Thou, O Lord, preservest man and beast.

Church speakers sometimes pick up local taxi messages. Recently, just as the minister said 'Amen' at the end of the prayers, the message boomed out through the speakers: 'Request understood and will be dealt with promptly!'

English Prayer	Scottish Reply
Grant that we may not be like porridge stiff, stodgy and hard to stir but like cornflakes crisp, fresh and ready to serve.	Grant that we may not be like cornflakes, lightweight, brittle and cold but like porridge, warm, comforting and full of natural goodness.

When called upon to deliver the offertory prayer, a deacon said: 'O Lord, why is it that a £10 note looks so large in the offering plate and so small in the grocer's?'

A Child's Prayer
'Bless Mummy and Daddy, but don't send them any more children...they don't know how to handle what they already have! If you send more...send them to my wonderful Grandmother!'

Don't you dare go above my head!

A boat crashed into rocks and began to sink.
'Does anybody know how to pray?' shouted the skipper.
'Yes I do,' said a zealous Christian, leaping to his feet.
'Good,' said the skipper.
'You pray. The rest of us will put on life-jackets. We're one short.

A young girl getting ready for bed interrupted a family gathering in the living-room. She said, 'I'm going to say my prayers now, does anybody want anything?' Then starting to pray, she said, 'Bless Mummy, Daddy and Grandma and Grandad and please God take care of yourself, because if anything happens to you we're all sunk!'

Preachers

During a long-winded sermon a mother was having some difficulty with a fractious child and decided to take the child out.
The preacher stopped speaking and said to the mother, 'Don't feel you have to leave, the child doesn't annoy me.'
'Maybe not,' said the mother, 'but you sure annoy it!'

A young cleric bounded up the pulpit steps full of confidence. His sermon, however, was a disaster, and he came down the steps bowed and humbled. An old man said to him, 'If tha'd gone up as tha came down, tha'd have come down as tha went up.'

A good sermon should be like a mini-skirt: short enough to be interesting yet long enough to cover the subject.

Two churchwardens were comparing the sermons of the curate and the vicar.
'Personally, I prefer the curates,' said one.
'Why's that?' asked the other.
'Well, the curate always says 'in conclusion' and concludes,' replied the first 'and the vicar always says 'lastly and lasts.'

A priest, carried away during a sermon cried out 'Lord give them pure hearts, Lord, give them clean hearts, give them sweet hearts'.

The perfect Minister preaches for exactly 15 minutes; he condemns sin but never upsets anyone. He works from 8.00 am until midnight and is also a good caretaker. He receives about £50 per week, wears good clothes, never looks shabby, keeps his diary up to date, entertains regularly, drives a new car and gives about £2,500 a year to the poor and to the congregation. His is 28-30 years old and has approximately 25-30 years parish experience. He has a burning desire to work with teenagers and spends all his time with senior citizens. The perfect minister smiles all the time with a straight face because he has a sense of humour that keeps him seriously dedicated at all times to his work. He makes daily calls on congregation families, shut-ins, and those in hospital; he spends all his time evangelising the unchurched and is always in his office when needed.

Taken from a Computer Survey.

'The subject of my sermon today,' said the Minister is:
'The milk of human kindness.'
A voice could be heard from the back of the church—'condensed, I hope!'

The preacher introduced his sermon with these words:
'Now before I start I want to say something...'

A vicar used to preach very short sermons, frequently ending with a few words that people remembered long afterwards. Here are some of his ear-catching words:
'Most people wish to serve God—but only in an advisory capacity.'
'When it comes to giving, some people stop at nothing.'
'There is no room for God in a man who is full of himself'.

Critical member of the congregation to the preacher who read his sermon from notes:
'If you can't remember it, how do you expect us to?'

Preaching about Adam and Eve the vicar lost his notes and rummaged about amongst his pages as he spoke, 'and Adam said to Eve...Adam said to Eve...said to Eve...There appears to be a leaf missing!'

The new vicar had preached his first sermon but a sudden emergency had prevented one of the churchwardens from attending church that day. When the churchwarden saw the vicar during the week, the following conversation took place:
Churchwarden: 'I was so sorry to have missed your first sermon, Vicar.'
Vicar: with great modesty: 'Oh, you didn't miss much.'
Churchwarden: 'So they tell me.'

In the 'good old days' the chapel was heated by a combustion stove in the centre of the room on which stood a whistling kettle. Just as the preacher finished his sermon, the whistle blew. The preacher said, That's a good idea.;
The steward replied, 'With the type of preacher we sometimes get I only half fill it.'

There was a well-known Methodist local preacher who lived in Porthleven and was very short. One Sunday morning he was preaching at Helston Wesley Chapel and because the pulpit was so high, stood on an orange box. He announced, 'My text is—A little while you see me and in a little while you will see me not.'
Just at that point the orange box gave way and he disappeared from sight.

A pre-sermon prayer:
'Lord fill my mouth with worthwhile stuff,
and nudge me when I've said enough.'

A minister was giving the address at a Yale University Graduation ceremony. Using Yale as his theme, he spoke for 15 minutes on **Y** for youth, 10 minutes on **A** for ambition and 12 minutes on **L** for loyalty. He had just launched into **E** for endeavour when a student whispered, 'I'm glad I don't go to the Massachusetts Institute of Technology.'

The vicar was preaching a powerful sermon concerning Death and Judgement. In the course of the sermon he said. 'To think that all of you living in this parish will one day die.'
A man in the front pew started laughing and when the vicar sternly said, 'My good man, why do you find such a serious subject so funny?' the man replied, 'Ha, Ha! Vicar I don't live in this parish.'

'Many preachers have a good head of steam and a fine train of thought but they lack terminal facilities…'

Churchgoer to Vicar: 'Your sermon reminded me of the mercies of God. I thought it would endure forever.'

A preacher whose sermon had gone down very badly asked a parson who was in his congregation afterwards:
'How would you have delivered that sermon?'
The visiting priest, after a moment's thought said,
'Under an assumed name!'

Then there is the one about the preacher who was disturbed by the snoring of grandad in the front pew. He stopped and asked a choirboy to wake him up. The lad promptly replied, 'You wake him up…you put him to sleep.'

'In the beginning,' said the preacher, 'Adam blamed Eve, Eve blamed the serpent and the serpent hadn't got a leg to stand on.'

As a student we often took services in a Baptist chapel at Hawksbridge, near Keighley. Our hosts were always Mr and Mrs Laycock, who fed students like princes with enormous portions of beef and Yorkshire Pudding. Then two hours later, after a snooze in front of the fire, it was time for tea with mountains of sandwiches and piles of jelly.

One student refused his tea saying he'd have indigestion and be unable to preach. Later, after evening service the student thanked his hosts most profusely.

Mr Laycok replied, 'its been nice having you young man—but having heard the sermon, tha might as well've 'ad thi tea!'

Questions

What are the steps to take on meeting a large lion?
Very big ones.

If two's company and three's a crowd, what's four and five?
Nine.

What do you call a cat who's swallowed a duck?
A duck-filled fatty puss.

Where was King Solomon's temple?
At one side of his head.

Can I try on that blue suit in the window?
No, sir. You'll have to use the changing room like everyone else.

What does an agnostic, dyslexic insomniac do?
He lies awake at night and wonders if there is a dog?

What is the difference between a cat and a comma?
A cat has claws at the end of its paws; a comma has a pause at the end of it's clause.

What is sandpaper?
A map of the desert.

Who rides a camel and carried a lamp?
Florence of Arabia.

What do you call a nun with a washing machine?
Sister Matic

Who was the last saint to get into heaven?
St Justin

What do gorillas sing at Christmas?
Jungle Bells, Jungle Bells.

Which king invented fractions?
Richard the Third.

The ruler of Russia was called the Tsar, and his wife was the Tsarina. What were their children called?
Tzardines

Rejoice and Sing

For years one congregation were reluctant to sing the hymn 'Awake our souls, away our fears' by Isaac Watts. This was because of the line in the last verse 'Swift as the eagle cuts the air.'
A respected but somewhat sensitive church member was a Mr Eagle and he was the local barber!

From a church service sheet:
Solo: Death where is they sting?
Hymn: Search me, O God.

I don't care if communion will clash with the European Cup-Final. Take it down.

The Presbyterians don't like the hymn 'Stand up, stand up for Jesus' because it might give offence to the disabled.
But what a precedent.
'Hark the glad sound' could offend the deaf,
'Lift up thine eyes' is an insult to the blind,
'Brother clasps the hand of brother, is sexist,
'Fight the good fight' provokes aggression,
'I will stand upon my watch' upsets watchmakers,
'Who fixed this floating ball' questions the work of plumbers,
and what of the poor father who at his daughters wedding had to sing, 'Be present awful father to give away this bride.'

Shopping

The curate's wife had just returned from a visit to the sales with a smart two-piece outfit. Her husband remonstrated with her, saying that they could not afford it.
She replied that she appreciated the fact, but the outfit had been a bargain and she had been tempted.
'In that case', said her husband, 'you should have said "get thee behind me Satan"'. 'Oh, but I did' said his wife, 'and that was when Satan said "It's a perfect fit at the back madam."'

An old lady watched a young man at the Chatsworth House Shopping area as he moved items about with great energy.
'What are you doing?' She asked.
'Making a new display area', he replied. The old woman called back to her friend, 'Hear that Gladys? He's making a nudist play area!'

Someone asking for a copy of the Church Times was told by the newsagent: 'It isn't in yet. Some of the other comics are late, too.'

Chemist handing prescription to a customer: 'Take one of these every four hours. Or as often as you can get the lid off'.

Customer to television salesman:
'I don't need remote control.
With four kids, my chances of controlling it are already remote.'

A launderette and a religious bookshop agreed a joint name for their adjoining premises. They called it: 'Cleanliness is next to Godliness.'

'Boycott the new launderette!' the shocked old lady told her friends.
'Why? Just read the notice above the machines.'
WHEN THE LIGHT GOES OUT PLEASE REMOVE ALL YOUR CLOTHES.

A Sunday School teacher was shopping in a supermarket when she spotted a man she thought she knew. After hailing him warmly she realised she was mistaken; attempting to cover her confusion she said: 'I'm sorry, I thought you were the father of one of my children.'

The wife of a gynaecologist, was walking down a crowded supermarket aisle when she was approached by an excited stranger who loudly proclaimed, 'I just have to tell you how much I adore your husband.' He got me pregnant when no one else could!'

Man: 'Can I have a parrot for my son?'
Pet shop owner: 'Sorry, sir, we don't do swaps.'

After browsing through the haberdashery at a department store a customer asked, 'Do you have any invisible thread?' The assistant replied, 'I haven't seen any', and then added, 'What does it look like?'

'I'd like some nails please', said a customer at the ironmongers.
'Yes sir, how long do you want them?'
'I'd like to keep them please.'

Spoonerisms

The Reverend William Archibald Spooner was the Warden of New College, Oxford. He was a nervous man who had trouble getting his words to come out straight. In church one Sunday, Spooner told his congregation, 'Let us sing, The Kingering Congs their Tattles Tike,' The hymn was, The Conquering Kings their Titles take.

On another occasion he announced the next hymn would be from Iceland's Greasy Mountain.

At a wedding he told the groom, 'It is kistomary to cuss the bride.'

Speaking to a group of farmers he intended to greet them as 'sons of toil,' but said 'I see before me tons of soil.'

Sport

A vicar was given out LBW in a vital church cricket match.
'That wasn't out umpire,' he shouted.
'Don't you think so?' said the umpire. 'Have a look in tonight's newspaper.'

A Yorkshire groundsman at a charity football match commented, 'It was a poor turn out. There were a lot o' folk theer as nivver turned up.'

Patient: 'Doctor, everbody thinks I'm crazy about cricket.'

Doctor: 'How that?'

Patient: 'Oh no! Not you as well!'

Sunday

The Vicar's not been the same since the Sunday Trading Laws changed

Taxation

A new Christian wrote to the Inland Revenue, 'I can't sleep at night so I am enclosing £100 I forgot to declare. P.S. If I still can't sleep I will send the rest.'

Discussing the environment with his friend, one man asked, 'Which of our natural resources do you think will become exhausted first?'
'The taxpayer', answered the other.

Standing by the Wailing Wall in Jerusalem, the Jewish guide said, 'We have two such walls in Israel. This one here and another at the tax office'.

Temperance

One Sunday the preacher—a keen abstainer—proclaimed that all beer and spirits should be thrown into the river. The choir then sang lustily: 'Shall we gather at the river'.

Today's Sermon:
How much can a man drink?
With hymns from a full choir.

Coming to the end of his talk the temperance leader dramatically dropped a worm into a glass of whisky where it promptly withered. 'There', he cried, 'What does that prove?'
A hand went up immediately with the answer following, 'If you drink plenty of whisky, you'll never get worms!'

Third World

There was this family in Ethiopia, starving to death.
All mankind prayed: 'Save them Lord!' So the Lord sent a surplus of wheat to Kansas—they burnt it. So the Ethiopians grew thinner and mankind prayed: 'Lord, feed them!' So He sent a beef mountain to Brussels—they burnt it. So more Ethiopians died of hunger and the vultures picked over their corpses, and the world was shocked at the pictures.
Then mankind prayed: 'Lord, how can you allow such suffering?'

Dream of the Third World Child
I swam in your wine-lake,
Till, sated and warm,
I drunkenly staggered
To a subsidised farm.
I rolled in fresh butter
Which I'd not seen before,
Then I climbed your meat mountain
And ate more and more.
Till I woke, cold and hungry,
for you haven't the price
In your overstocked larders
Of a small bowl of rice.

One fifth of the world's 5.6 billion population is living in extreme poverty.
One third of the world's children are undernourished.
Half of the world's population lacks regular access to the most essential drugs.
12.2 million children under five die every year—95% from poverty-related illness.
More than half a million mothers die in childbirth.
More than one million children die of measles each year.
Vaccines to save them would cost 9p each.
More than half a million babies die of tetanus every year.

Tourists

A large American car pulled up outside the Parish Church. The old Verger was busy cutting the grass. The car window was wound down and a voice with a strong American accent called: 'Say, any great men born around these parts?' 'Nope', came the reply, 'only babies!'

At General Synod the Archbishop of Canterbury said, 'I receive letters of complaint over entrance fees for Cathedrals but a letter the other day complained that visitors could not tour a particular Cathedral because a large service was taking place! And the Dean of Canterbury received a letter from a group of American tourists who complained that when they visited the Cathedral they could not look over the building because it was full of worshippers. It was Christmas Day'.

Murphy was flying in a plane for the first time and was very frightened.
'Don't worry,' said a priest sitting alongside him. 'Have a nip of this,' and pulled a little flask from his pocket.
'Gee that's something,' said Murphy.
'Have another drop,' said the priest.
'That's the strongest stuff I've ever tasted,' said Murphy.
'It's the wine the Holy Father himself drinks,' confided the priest.
'S'trewth,' said Murphy, 'no wonder they carry him round in a chair!'

In Tel Aviv a tourist was about to enter the impressive Mann Auditorium to hear a concert by the Israel Philharmonic.
As he admired the architecture, he turned to his escort to ask if the building was named after Thomas Mann, the famous author.
'No,' said his friend. 'It's named after Frederic Mann from Philadelphia.'
'Never heard of him,' replied the tourist, 'what did he write?'
'A cheque.'

A woman in the airport toilets said to a woman beside her, 'I had nothing but trouble with the car getting here, it broke down on the motorway and a mechanic fitted a new battery but it broke down again two minutes later. Now I've just phoned my husband at home and he told me the dishwasher had packed up.'

'Excuse me,' chipped in another woman, 'do you mind telling me which flight you're on!'

'Look Dad, look,' cried the youngster excitedly as the customs officer chalked a tick on the holiday suitcase. 'He's given up looking for it!'

A somewhat cocky southern gent was driving in the Yorkshire Dales and he got lost looking for Ayesgarth Falls. Eventually he stopped and asked a local the way.
'There's a signpost half a mile down't road,' he said.
Being a bit clever, the motorist said, 'But I can't read'.
'Well it'll suit thee then', said the local, 'cos there's nowt on it.'

Toys

Did you hear about the teddy bear who got a job on the council digging holes in the road?
Monday was fine
Tuesday better and the hole got bigger
But on Wednesday he got to work and found that his pick had been stolen so he went to the boss to explain that he couldn't work without his pick.
The boss said, 'Don't worry about it—its Wednesday—today's the day the teddy bears have their picks nicked!'

Johnny had a teddy bear with a squint. A lady asked him the teddy's name and he said, 'Gladly'.
'Why do you call him Gladly?'
'He is named after the hymn: 'Gladly my cross-eyed bear'.

Vicars—Priests—Ministers

If his sermon is long—'He sends us to sleep.'
If it is short—'He hasn't bothered preparing.'
If his voice is raised in emotion—'He's shouting.'
If he speaks softly—'You can't hear him.'
If he's away—'Another holiday.'
If he's always at his home church—'He doesn't get out and see the world.'
If he's visiting—'He's never at home.'
If he's always at home—'He never visits anyone.'
If he talks about money—'He's too worldly.'
If he doesn't—'His feet aren't on the ground.'
If he organises lots of events—'He burns everyone out.'
If he doesn't—'There's no social diversion in our church.'
If he spends time talking to individuals—'He has his favourites.'
If he doesn't—'He never listens to people.'
If he wants to smarten up the church buildings—'He's always spending money.'
If he doesn't—'He's letting the place fall into disrepair.'
If he's young—'He lacks experience.'
If he's old—'He's past it.'
If he's single—'He doesn't know what true family life is like.'
If he's married with a family—'His loyalties are torn.'
If he's a she—'It'll cause a split in the church.'
If he's not—'We should be moving with the times!'
And if he dies?
'Nobody can ever take his place—'He was a wonderful man!'

Quote from a northern parish magazine: 'I am sure you will not wish to overwork our visiting priest while I am away and will keep funerals to a minimum.

'Come on Robin,' said his mother, 'finish your breakfast or you'll be late for church.'
'I don't want to go to church,' said Robin.
'But you must,' said his mother.
'The Sunday School teachers hate me,' said Robin.
'Even so...' said his mother.
'The children too, they hate me as well.'
'You still have to go,' said his mother.
'But why must I,' wailed Robin.
'Well,' said his mother, 'for one thing you're 55 years old and for another, you're the vicar!'

Chain Letter for the Perfect Minister

The perfect Minister preaches for only ten minutes, but feeds his flock richly.

He condemns sin in general but not in particular for fear of offending.

He works from 8 am until midnight and is also the church caretaker.

He earns £50 per week, wears good clothes and drives a good car, buys good books and clothes his family, gives £20 per week to the church.

He is 29-years-old but has forty years' experience.

He makes 15 house visits a day but is always in the vestry for consultation.

If your minister does not measure up, simply send this letter to six other churches that are tired of theirs. Then bundle up your minister and send him to the church at the top of the list. In one week you will receive 1,643 ministers and one of them should be suitable.

Have faith in this letter—one church broke the chain and got its old minister back in less than three weeks.

From a Vicar's Vestry:
When in charge, ponder,
When in trouble, delegate,
When in doubt, mumble.

'Out, LBW,' cried the umpire at the charity cricket match.
Disgruntled, the vicar shouldered his bat and walked towards the pavilion.
'You need glasses, giving me out like that,' he grumbled, passing a man in a white coat.
'So do you,' came the reply,
'I'm selling ice-cream.'

The priest who joined our class in medicine at the University of Cape Town invariably wore his clerical clothes and dog-collar. One day, when we were in our hospital year of study, he turned up in ordinary dress.

'It's the patients,' he explained. 'Every time I approach them, they think they're going to die.'

A penurious curate of Wath,
His cassock much eaten by moth,
Cried 'Lord, hear my prayer,
Do not let your fresh ayer
Freeze the kneeze of your Man of the Cloth'.

Weddings

*Did you hear of the bride who wanted to make sure that she did
the right thing when entering the church on her Wedding Day?
She kept saying to herself, 'Aisle'; 'Altar'; 'Hymn'.*

A bridegroom was so nervous that he spluttered out, 'I will', three times,
twice in the wrong places. When the bride and groom eventually got to
the vestry to sign the register the vicar congratulated the groom and
hoped he and his bride would be very happy.
The bridegroom stammered back, 'Same to your sir and many of 'em.'

I don't care if United are at home. You're the Groom!

Work

'Are you self-motivated?' asked a boss interviewing the teenage girl for a job. 'No, I'm afraid not,' she replied. 'I have to catch the bus.'

> **Why is it that so many people engage in do-it-yourself at home and let-somebody-else-do-it at work?**

There was a decorator who cheated his customers by charging them for paint which he then watered down. But, finally, he carried the whole process so far that even the most short-sighted client would see how patchy it was.

'What can I do?' he cried—and from heaven came a great voice booming: 'Repaint and thin no more!'

Is that the only reference you can come up with?

Come to think of it Vicar, you've not been in my shop much either!

Businessman. I'm going to sack that chauffer—three times he's nearly killed me.

Wife. O Darling, give him just one more chance

Work Study

A company Chairman had been given tickets to the performance of Schubert's unfinished symphony. He couldn't go, and passed them on to his work study consultant. The next morning, the chairman asked him how he had enjoyed the performance and was handed a memorandum which read:

'For considerable periods, the four oboe players had nothing to do. The number should be reduced, and their work spread over the whole orchestra, thus eliminating peaks of inactivity.

All of the 12 violins were playing identical notes. This seemed unnecessary duplication, and the staff of this section should be dramatically cut.

Much effort was absorbed in the playing of demi semi-quavers. Now this seems an excessive refinement, and it is recommended that all notes should be rounded up to the nearest semi-quaver.

No useful purpose is served by repeating with horns the passage that had already been played by the strings. If all such redundant passages were eliminated, the concert could be reduced from two hours to twenty minutes.

If Schubert had attended to those matters, he would probably have been able to finish his symphony after all.'

Young People

It used to be that growing up meant getting all your questions answered... now it means getting all your answers questioned.

Have you ever noticed that if you pass your exams everyone says that you get your brains from your parents, but if you fail they all say you're stupid.

The young people in our church decided to raise money by having a car wash. However, on the morning the car wash was to be held, it was pouring with rain. The vicar saved the day by putting up this sign: God's Co-operative Car Wash. We Wash—He Rinses.

'I must say he's a bit different".

The Real Delinquents

We read in the papers, we hear on the air,
Of killing and stealing and crime everywhere.
We sigh and we say, as we notice the trend,
'This young generation, where will it all end?'
But can we be sure that it's their fault alone?
That maybe most if it is really our own:
Too much money to spend, too much idle time,
Too many movies of passion and crime.
Too many books not fit to be read,
Too many children encouraged to roam,
By too many parents who won't stay at home.

Kids don't make the movies, they don't write the books,
That paint a gay picture of gangsters and crooks.
They don't make the liquor, they don't run the bars,
They don't make the laws, they don't all drive cars.
They don't make the drugs that addle the brain,
It's all done by older folks, greedy for gain.
Thus, in many cases, it must be confessed,
The label 'Delinquent' fits older folks best.

YOU'VE GOT TO
LAUGH.....